Quilt Your Favorite Photos

Shoot It   Sketch It   Stitch It

Betty Alofs

©2006 Betty Alofs
Published by

kp krause publications

An Imprint of F+W Publications

700 East State Street • Iola, WI 54990-0001
715-445-2214 • 888-457-2873

Our toll-free number to place an order or obtain a free catalog is (800) 258-0929.

The following registered trademark terms and companies appear in this publication:
Lite Steam-a-Seam 2® Fusible Web, Sakura Pigma® Micron® Pens, Sharpie®, Sulky® of America, Sulky® Tear Easy™ Stabilizer, Ultrasuede®, The Warm™ Company, Warm & Natural® Batting

Library of Congress Catalog Number: 2005934369

ISBN 13: 978-0-89689-215-6
ISBN: 0-89689-215-8

Edited by Sarah Brown and Candy Wiza
Designed by Donna Mummery

Printed in China

dedication

I dedicate this to my students, who have been instrumental in encouraging me to continue with this retirement career and who have given me so much in return with their friendship and loyalty. I especially dedicate this to my sweet husband, who makes it possible for me to have this much fun doing what I love to do; he puts up with my many days away from home and my weeks of traveling, is proud of my accomplishments and encourages me to continue to enjoy this new direction in my life.

acknowledgments

Writing this book to share my methods has given me a great deal of satisfaction. I have enjoyed teaching classes while working on the book and its projects, and my students continue to teach me a great deal along the way.

I would like to express my gratitude to Jan Krentz, who has always been such a loyal and helpful friend, and who has shared many ideas and suggestions on how to organize and improve my design work. I admire her dedication to her own work and how she constantly inspires others with her influence.

I would also like to express my gratitude to Beckie Biddle, owner of Sowing Sisters Quilt and Artisan Center in Carlsbad, Calif., who kindly allowed me to use her classroom not only for classes, but for my personal workshops, and who has been a tireless promoter! And my thanks to Marcia Binkert of Jamul, Calif., a special friend who is, by her own definition, "my biggest fan." Thanks Marcia! I wouldn't want to forget my pattern instruction testers: Darlene Sweetwood and Susanne Fagot of El Cajon, Calif. They made me rethink my wording, explain unfamiliar terms more thoroughly and helped me walk through the processes more clearly.

My regards and thanks go to The Warm Co., Sulky of America and Pfaff Sewing Machines. The contributions from these companies have been instrumental in helping me finish my projects on time and with proficiency.

And last, but certainly not least, I would like to express my appreciation to Julie Stephani for her belief in my book concept. And, many thanks to Candy Wiza and Sarah Brown for their expertise in editing to keep me on target and for smoothing out my rough edges!

introduction

In 1999, after many years of quilting, teaching and learning more and more about the craft, I embarked on a personal mission to create a one-of-a-kind memorial pictorial quilt. This was quite an undertaking, littered with false starts, learning about new projects and techniques that made things easier and rejected patterns that were just too darn hard to make! Along the way, I discovered some techniques of my own that helped in the creation process. I explored the many tools and supplies that are available to quilters and artisans from all artistic disciplines. Quilt shops are usually the first stop in collecting the supplies, but I found that I could not overlook art stores, craft shops, scrapbooking shops, hobby shops and yes, even grocery stores (great source for cheesecloth).

My first effort was the "Celebrate San Diego" quilt made in 2000. It contains 13 blocks of realistic-looking subjects ranging from buildings (San Diego Mission, Point Loma Lighthouse, Hotel Del Coronado) to animals (giant pandas, orcas, California gray whale) to other scenes familiar to all San Diego residents and visitors alike.

I established my company, Betty A's Designs, to market the patterns at the urging of my friends.

This encouraged me to make more "city quilts." As I prepared the patterns and instructions, I decided to learn a little more about the subjects of my quilt and did some research at my local library. I included a little paragraph of history about the subject of each pattern. City quilts soon became an obsession; much like other aspects of quilting seems to with quilters in general. I created more quilts and was enjoying every minute of it, especially the required travel to photograph the subjects for my quilts.

The past five years of creating pictorial appliqué patterns has been a wonderful experience. I have enjoyed the journey, the new friendships made, the opportunity to tell other quilters about my quilting process and the students that are an unending source of inspiration, learning, friendship and loyalty. This book is a compilation of the journey toward learning how to create fabric renditions of photographs for quilts. It is satisfying to see your much-loved photograph come to life in fabric. It is a great remembrance of those people and places you hold dear. So grab your camera, visit your prized locations and begin your own journey to quilting your favorite photos!

Celebrate San Diego quilt.

CHAPTER 1
GETTING STARTED

This chapter outlines the process for making a pattern from your inspirational photograph. Your first assignment includes advice for acquiring the initial supplies, taking good photographs and selecting the right fabric for your quilt.

MATERIALS

- Camera and film (35mm or digital)
- Notepaper for making notes about the times of day, angles, etc., and for noting colors and textures of fabrics you will need
- Tripod for your camera (optional)
- Clear acetate or other clear plastic sheet

first assignment

1 Take several photos of your subject. Take them from different angles and at different times of the day. To achieve realism, it is important that the photograph has light and shadow to provide depth and proportion to the finished block. Try to take the photograph from a side angle, like the lighthouse quilt shown on page 10. This will give you more light and shadow areas. Take lots of pictures to give you a choice. *Note:* It is best to take the photo in full sunlight in the early morning or afternoon. Noon light falls from straight above and gives you few shadows, if any. Do not face the sun directly or you will experience a darker look in your photograph. Also, do not take the photograph with the sun directly behind you. This causes a washed-out look and your *own* shadow may be in the picture.

2 Develop your photos into the normal 4" x 6" size. If you use a digital camera, you can download the pictures to your computer and print them out as a regular page size. It is **not** a good idea to enlarge the picture too much on a copy machine because the outlines become fuzzy and you may lose some of the detail. Decide on a photo to use; you may even decide on a composite effect by using several pictures to make the view you want that includes all features, shadows and angles for the ideal appearance.

3 Trace your chosen photo onto clear acetate or some other clear plastic sheet. Enlarge the tracing using one of the methods in Chapter 2 on pages 19-23.

I combined two photos of my home to create the view I wanted.

The view above turned into a quilt featuring my home.

Once you have decided on a photo to replicate, it's time to choose the fabric. In this lighthouse example, the fabrics are based on the colors in the photo; I added other fabrics to brighten up the scene. The white picket fence is a difficult print to find in fabric, but, with a little creativity, I discovered a way to create the illusion of one. Since picket fences usually surround a grassy yard, I chose a green-and-white striped fabric and cut across the top with pinking shears to create the look of the top of the pickets. The flowers in front of the fence are there for color and added dimension. The fabrics selected for this block are shown on the next page. Make yourself a little chart like this one to help you put each fabric in its proper place on the block as you work.

Point Loma Lighthouse quilt.

White for house	Blue window reflection	Brown tree trunk
		Sparkly net for light tower
Black roof shadows	Dark for tower and door	Green bushes
Green grass	Green tree	Stripe for picket fence
Flowers	Gray for shadows	Dark gray for roof

Make a fabric chart to keep you organized as you work. This chart is for the quilt shown at left.

dark barn wood

silo (dark)

stones

flowers

grass

fabric choices

Consider the following when making your fabric choices:

- *Necessary details:* Examine each detail in the photograph and determine what is really necessary to make the block look real. For example, many homes and buildings have gutters that run under the eaves then down to the ground. Do you really need them in the quilt? Decide which angle looks best to you. How much foliage do you want around a building? You are now the artist, so if you find a particular portion of your photo is too intricate or detailed to duplicate, put a tree in front of it! Look at the windows to see if they are intricate or simple. How much detail do you want? Are curtains showing in the windows? You can add or subtract the details you want in your finished block. You can simplify parts of the picture and still maintain its integrity.

- *Landscaping:* You can create ideal landscaping in your quilt, even if your lawn at home is not quite as luxurious as you would like. One of my students was living in a brand new house that had not yet been landscaped. On her quilt, she created a flower garden on one side, planted some trees and bushes, created a winding slate pathway and added flowers on both sides, all on the wallhanging. When she showed the finished quilt to her husband, he loved how she created the landscape; so together, they re-created that landscape around their new home! In the lighthouse quilt shown on page 10, the fabrics are based on the colors in the photo; I added other fabrics to brighten up the scene.

- *Shadows:* Paying attention to the direction of the light source (where the light is coming from) and keeping it consistent throughout your quilt makes a big difference. The shadow should be in keeping with the light source. By selecting fabrics to represent that shading, you achieve realism in your quilt. Look at the shading in your photo. Your light source in an outdoor picture is the sun. From which direction is the sun coming? Look at the cast shadows, or shadows that are cast on the ground on or around the house, trees, fences, etc. Make sure the shadows you put in the final block are consistent with the light source.

Cartoonish clouds.

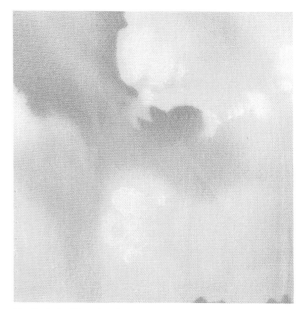

Realistic-looking clouds.

Realistic-looking clouds.

Sunburst with clouds.

Take your photograph with you to the quilt store or have it beside you as you shop on the Internet to help you determine which fabric will best depict the various areas in your picture. Many times you can use the back or wrong side of the fabric for a lighter value than the front. This, of course, is not true for all fabrics. Batiks sometimes look similar on the front as on the back. On the other hand, some fabric backs are very light because the pattern does not show through.

The amount of fabric you need for the assembly of the blocks is minimal. Just small pieces are used for the different parts of the blocks. The background sky and ground require at least a fat quarter (¼ yard measuring 18" x 22" instead of 9" x 44"), but it depends on how large you plan on making your block. The binding and backing will require ½ yard. Borders can generally be made with ½ yard as well, especially if you plan to miter the corners. Sashing and border materials depend on the size of the block you make, and whether you are going to make many blocks to put together into a large quilt. Information on determining your fabric yardages is listed with each project.

Remember the shadows we talked about? Well, now you need a fabric that will match that shadow. Shadows are not always dark gray or black. A shadow can reflect the colors around it. Some shadows are blue, some brown and some look very purple. Decide which colors and values your shadows represent, and look for that fabric.

The sky in your quilt is a good place to start choosing fabric. Manufacturers are now printing many different sky fabrics. Search for some that resemble the real sky, not one with "cartoon" clouds. Maybe you need a little color in the sky like when the sunset is just starting and the sky is taking on a lovely pink glow. Perhaps you like a clear sky or a foggy one. This is your choice, so look again at the photo and find the perfect sky fabric print.

The photos on page 13 are scans of sky fabrics. The first one shows clouds that are almost "cartoonish" because they are so perfectly formed. The others, all commercial fabrics, can be used realistically and the last one can be used for a dramatic sky. Look for sunset shades like those found in hand dyed fabrics.

Look at the trees around you. They are many shades of green, blue-green, gray-green, forest-green, jade, lime and yellow-green. Mix the various shades together like those in a natural setting. Fir trees can be "painted" with thread and a zigzag stitch. Tree trunk fabrics can be found in unsuspecting ways. Fabric that looks like a shake roof can be turned upside down to made a perfect palm tree trunk. Tree trunks can be whitish gray, brown, black or covered with moss. Grass is sometimes bright green and carpet-like, and sometimes shaggy and dark.

Use some commercial fabrics that simulate trees and bushes. They do not actually have to *be* tree fabrics, just look like them. Some are actually from paintings of trees, which is ideal for the projects in this book.

The search for fabrics is a lot of fun. Start your search with your own fabric stash. If you cannot find what you need there, you can visit your favorite quilt and fabric shops for new prints and colors.

Typical tree fabrics.

general tools and supplies

Appliqué pressing sheet: A silicone-coated, see-through plastic sheet.

Backing fabric: The amount will depend on the size of your quilt.

Batting: I use Warm & Natural by The Warm Co. It's flat, does not stretch easily and holds its shape well for wallhangings as well as bed quilts. It is easy to quilt through, whether by hand or machine, and will lay flat after quilting without distorting the quilt.

Clear overhead transparencies (write-on type), 8½" x 11" clear acetate or common clear sheet protectors: Use to trace your photo and enlarge it with the use of an overhead projector.

Drawing rulers that are thin clear plastic (not rotary cutting rulers): For refining your enlarged block pattern.

Enlarging tool: Choose one of the items below to enlarge your photo.
- ➤ Overhead projector: Used to project an acetate tracing onto a paper taped to the wall. Find at office supply stores, libraries or schools.
- ➤ ¼" clear plastic grid: Used to place over a photo to create separate sections that can be re-drawn on a larger-scale grid. Find at some quilt supply shops and on the Internet.
- ➤ Flatbed scanner: You can enlarge via the scanner copy feature. Find at computer and electronic stores.

Fabric spray adhesive: Used to adhere your fabric, batting and quilt top together to prepare for quilting (in lieu of pinning or basting).

Freezer paper: Find this by the roll at most grocery stores, and in packages of 8½" x 11" sheets at some quilt shops (sometimes called "appliqué template paper").

Fusible web: Choose the lightest weight available; it will not separate from the protective sheet until you peel it off. Its slight tackiness will allow you to place fused fabrics where you want them and will keep them in place until you either remove and replace them or iron them down permanently.

Glass head pins: These won't melt under the heat of the iron.

Hot iron cleaner: Keep this product on hand in case you get a little fusible on your iron. While the iron is hot, place a small amount on a piece of folded muslin; run the iron over the muslin in a circular motion. After the plate of the iron is cleaned, turn the muslin over and run the iron on an unused section to remove any residue from the cleaner. Find at fabric stores, quilt shops, craft stores and grocery stores.

Iron and ironing surface: Small travel irons and reversible (cut and press) mats work well.

Permanent fine point markers: These pens will write on the acetate or transparency without smearing.

Scissors: You will need a pair that can cut fabric or paper; you will be cutting fused fabrics with freezer paper on top.

Sewing machine: You will need one with the following feet:

➤ Open toe embroidery foot
➤ Couching foot
➤ ¼" foot
➤ Free-motion foot

Stabilizer: Available in tear-away, dissolvable and leave-in. I prefer the tear-away stabilizer (see Resources on page 126).

Threads: Have your choice of cotton, embroidery, monofilament or metallic threads on hand. Use cotton for general seaming, decorative stitching and outlining with satin stitch. Use embroidery rayon thread, which has a sheen, for a sparkly effect. Use monofilament, which is clear and very fine, where you want no thread showing; use clear for white and light fabrics and the smoke color for dark and black fabrics.

Tweezers: Use to place your small fused pieces.

White Paper (at least 11" x 17"): Cut or tape to the size you want your finished block.

OPTIONAL SUPPLIES

Netting, netting with sparkles, lamé, tulle, organdy, opalescent organdy, lace, crystals, beads, yarn, buttons. Let your imagination soar! Look for specialty items in scrapbook shops. Check out your local craft stores. Another good source is an educational store, one that specializes in products for school teachers. Regular quilt and fabric shops have a wealth of embellishments. Look at the pattern catalogs in a fabric store, they contain many useable ideas. Visit bead shops, yarn shops, embroidery specialty shops, where you can find many inspirational ideas.

glossary of terms

Couching: Sewing over a piece of thick floss or yarn with a zigzag stitch to hold it in place.

Couching foot: A presser foot for your sewing machine that has a small hole in the foot for threading the floss or yarn into to keep it in place as you sew over it. Couching can be accomplished with or without the couching foot.

Fat quarter: A ¼ yard of fabric that is 18" x 22" (instead of the usual measurement of 9" x 44"). It is made by cutting ½ yard of fabric (18" by 44") in half. A fat quarter is a wider piece of fabric that is easier to use than a typical 9"-wide piece.

Fussy cut: Cutting out a motif from a printed fabric to appliqué onto another fabric. The technique of Broderie Perse utilized this method for creating medallions and bouquets by layering individually cut motifs on a background and hand appliquéing them in place. For the projects in this book, apply the fusible web to the fabrics' wrong side first; then cut out the motif.

Mitered corner: A 45-degree angle cut on a straight fabric border. It is especially attractive and gives the border the look of a frame.

Open toe or embroidery foot: Sometimes called a darning foot, this is a presser foot in the shape of an upside-down "U." The open part of the "U" faces the front, where the lines being sewn can be seen clearly.

Rough cut: Cut approximately ¼" or more away from the edge of the motif. You will cut on traced lines or exact edges of a motif later in the process.

Thread painting: Free-motion sewing to create texture on your piece. Use this technique to enhance an already printed design or texture, and to create vines, weeds, blades of grass, branches and other additional embellishments.

Triple stitch or reinforced stitch: An optional stitch found on most newer sewing machines that provides a thicker sewing line. The stitch goes one stitch forward, one back and one forward, then again, forward, back, forward, making three stitches, one on top of the other.

Walking foot: A special attachment available for most machines, and is built-in on some (called the Integrated Dual Feed on the Pfaff). It feeds the fabric from the top and bottom at the same time, keeping all layers of the project aligned and preventing stretching of the top layer.

CHAPTER 2

MAKING THE PATTERN

Now we really get to work! There are many ways to make a pattern and this is my favorite method. Familiarize yourself with the basic technique for making a pattern, and the rest will fall into place. I will describe four different methods to enlarge your drawing, and follow up with the placement order numbering system. This will help you to organize your work as you construct your block(s).

size the pattern

Your pattern should be life-size. In other words, it should be the size you want your finished quilt to be. Make the size decision before you begin making your pattern. Generally speaking, a size of about 24" high x 36" wide is a good wallhanging size for a building such as your home or a landmark. It is small enough to make the backing in one piece and manipulate in your sewing machine for the quilting, but large enough to enable you to put in all the little details that make your pattern unique. Other sizes, such as 18" wide x 24" high, work well for a taller, narrower building. You can enlarge your original photograph a bit in a copy machine, or on your scanner, but if you enlarge it too much, the details become fuzzy and the sharp outline is lost. Therefore it is better to trace the original photo before enlarging. There are several ways to enlarge the tracing of the photo.

Method 1:
Use Clear Plastic to Trace and an Overhead Projector to Enlarge

1 Place your photo on a firm surface like a tabletop, cover with a piece of clear acetate, plastic sheet protector or clear write-on overhead transparency. Tape the clear sheet down to the table so it will not shift as you trace.

2 Using a fine-point permanent marker, trace your subject onto the plastic (regular felt-tip pens will smear and ball-point pens and pencils will not work). Don't worry about every little detail; some are too small to re-create in a pattern, and you can add others later. But be sure to trace around the shadows so you will be aware of their correct location.

3 Tape a large piece of white paper (can be freezer paper from a roll or white wrapping paper) on a blank wall. Roughly draw a box (square or rectangle) the size you have decided to make your finished pattern.

4 Place the tracing onto the overhead projector faceplate. Project the image onto the paper, moving the projector toward the wall or away from the wall to adjust the image to fit inside the box you have drawn. Adjust the focus on the projector to make the image as sharp as possible.

5 Follow all the lines that are projected onto the paper using the fine-point permanent marker. *Note:* It is difficult to follow the lines absolutely straight since you will be standing at an angle and you are holding your arm up for a long time. Don't worry; to make your final pattern, you will trace it again on a clean piece of paper, this time using rulers to help you get the lines perfectly straight where they need to be straight, and curve gently where appropriate.

6 Take the paper off the wall and place it on a flat surface. Cover your paper with a clean piece of good white paper, taping the edges together to keep them from shifting.

7 Place the two layers of paper on a light box, light table or bright window (see supply list) where you can see the drawing through the top layer of paper. If you can see the drawing through the good white paper without the help of a light box, light table or window, no light box will be required.

8 Trace the lines onto the good white paper, using rulers to draw straight lines. This is your finished pattern! See page 24 to number the pattern pieces.

Use transparencies with an overhead projector.

Slip the photo inside a sheet protector and trace directly on it with a fine-point permanent marker.

Method 2:
Use Clear Plastic to Trace and a Copy Machine to Enlarge

1 Place your photo on a firm surface like a tabletop, cover it with a piece of clear acetate, plastic sheet protector or clear write-on overhead transparency. Tape the clear sheet down to the table so it will not shift as you trace.

2 Using a fine-point permanent marker, trace your subject onto the plastic (regular felt-tip pens will smear and ball-point pens and pencils will not work). Don't worry about every little detail; some are too small to re-create in a pattern, and you can add others later. But be sure to trace around the shadows so you will be aware of their correct location.

3 Take the tracing to a copy shop for enlargement. First, make a same size copy on white paper. Then, depending on the size you want your finished quilt to be, there are several ways to determine the percentage for enlargement:

● One is by using good old math! Here is the formula to calculate the enlargement percentage. *Note:* The dimensions should be in decimals. Rounding up to the nearest decimal will work fine. Also, some copy machines only copy up to 200 percent. In this case, enlarge once, and then use the formula again to enlarge until you have the desired size.

➤ (Desired dimension) ÷ (present dimension) x 100 = enlargement percentage

➤ For example, if you want your pattern to be 24" high and it is presently 6.5" high, the formula will look like this:

➤ 24 ÷ 6.5 = 3.69

➤ 3.69 x 100 = 369 percent enlargement

● Another method is to purchase a proportional scale from an art supply shop. This is a plastic tool with two circles joined at the centers. The outside circle has the dimensions for the final size desired, and the inside circle shows the current dimensions of the object you want to enlarge. The little window in the inside circle shows percentages. Move the inside circle so that the current measurement aligns with the desired measurement on the outside circle. Once the two measurements are aligned, the percentage for enlargement shows in the window. I find this tool invaluable!

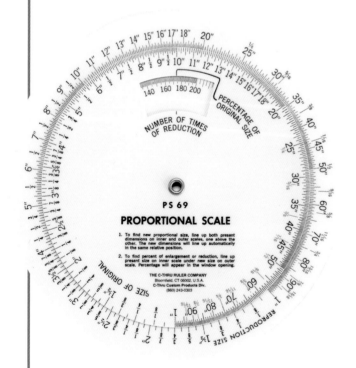

Typical proportional scale.

4 After finding the percentage of enlargement, take your tracing to a copy or print shop. If it is a self-service shop, you can punch in the enlargement percentage yourself. If not, ask the clerk to enlarge your tracing by the percentage you require to arrive at your desired size.

5 Place your enlarged tracing on a flat surface. Cover your tracing with a clean piece of good white paper, taping the edges together to keep them from shifting.

6 Place the two layers of paper on a light box, light table or bright window (see supply list) where you can see the drawing through the top layer of paper. If you can see the drawing through the good white paper without the help of a light box, light table or window, no light box will be required.

7 Trace the lines onto the good white paper, using rulers to draw straight lines. This is your finished pattern! See page 24 to number the pattern pieces.

Another method is to use carbon paper between your photo and the clean sheet of paper. Using a ball-point pen, trace the parts of the photo you want. Then take the carbon tracing and refine it before having it enlarged by the copy shop.

Method 3:
Use Clear Plastic to Trace and a Scanner to Enlarge

1 Place your photo on a firm surface like a tabletop, cover with a piece of clear acetate, plastic sheet protector or clear write-on overhead transparency. Tape the clear sheet to the table so it will not shift as you trace.

2 Using a fine-point permanent marker, trace your subject onto the plastic (regular felt-tip pens will smear and ball-point pens and pencils will not work). Don't worry about every little detail; some are too small to re-create in a pattern, and you can add others later. But be sure to trace around the shadows so you will be aware of their correct location.

3 Place the tracing on the scanner bed and copy the tracing at 100 percent. This will give you a clean tracing on white paper.

4 Place the white copy on the scanner bed. Use the percentage for enlargement instructions from Method 2. If you are enlarging to a size greater than the size of your printer paper, you have several options. Some computers have a program where the enlarged drawing will be divided into sections, and it will print out each section separately. Tape the sections together to make the whole image. If this is not possible with your computer, cut your tracing into 2" squares and enlarge each one separately; then tape the sections together.

5 Place your enlarged tracing on a flat surface. Cover your tracing with a clean piece of good white paper, taping the edges together to keep them from shifting.

6 Place the two layers of paper on a light box, light table or bright window (see supply list) where you can see the drawing through the top layer of paper. If you can see the drawing through the good white paper without the help of a light box, light table or window, no light box will be required.

7 Trace the lines onto the good white paper, using rulers to draw straight lines. This is your finished pattern! See page 24 to number the pattern pieces.

Method 4:
Use the Grid Method to Enlarge

1 Place clear acetate or a plastic sheet protector over your photo. Using a fine-point permanent marker, draw vertical and horizontal grid lines ¼" apart. This will divide the photo into ¼"-square cells. Each cell has a portion of the photo.

2 On a large piece of white newsprint or other paper, draw vertical and horizontal grid lines 2" apart. Make sure you have the same number of cells (vertically and horizontally) as the photo grid.

3 Sketch each cell from the photo grid into a corresponding cell on the large paper grid. Select the cell in the first column and the first row of the grid over the picture. If there is something in that cell, sketch it into the corresponding large paper grid cell. Do the same with the next cell. Continue with each cell until finished. Some cells in the small grid have nothing in them, perhaps just background sky; ignore them and continue with the cells that have something to sketch.

4 Place your enlarged tracing on a flat surface. Cover your tracing with a clean piece of good white paper, taping the edges together to keep them from shifting.

5 Place the two layers of paper on a light box, light table or bright window (see supply list) where you can see the drawing through the top layer of paper. If you can see the drawing through the good white paper without the help of a light box, light table or window, no light box will be required.

6 Trace the lines onto the good white paper, using rulers to draw straight lines. This is your finished pattern! See page 24 to number the pattern pieces.

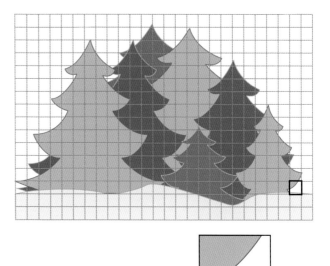

SCALE

The grid lines on the photo (which you will draw on clear plastic) are ¼" apart. The grid lines on the enlargement are 2" apart. So, ¼" equals 2" on the enlargement. This means that if you start with a photo that is 4" wide, you will have 16 grid cells, ¼" wide. Your enlargement will then have 16 grid cells, 2" wide. This will result in the larger pattern being 32" wide. This is a good, workable size for a wallhanging. Add one or more borders to increase the size. To make a smaller wallhanging, make the grid lines 1½" apart (this would make the pattern 24" wide).

tip... Look for clear plastic with a printed grid at art supply shops or office supply stores. Some quilt and craft shops also carry these handy grids. Check these Web sites, also:
- www.bighornquilts.com
- www.ezquilt.com/products
- www.joann.com/catalog

number the pattern pieces

Look at the drawing you have just completed. Would you like to add any more details? Can some details be ignored? Should there be more foliage than is really there to provide some color and interest? This is the chance to landscape the way you *think* it should look! The Point Loma Lighthouse is actually sitting atop a high peninsula, and has very little landscaping — just weeds and dirt — the way it appeared when it was an operating lighthouse. Adding some trees and flowers gave it some charm. This is called *artistic license,* and you can do the same to your block. Once you have completed adding or subtracting, you have a finished pattern ready to be numbered.

This numbering system tells you which appliqué piece will be placed down first, followed by all the rest in numbered sequence. Pieces will not butt up against each other, but will overlap. Therefore, when you are preparing the individual pattern pieces, some will be a little larger on one edge to give the next piece a place in which to adhere. All pieces will have to overlap or be overlapped by another piece. This is important so that all the pieces will become one intact unit.

1 Number each individual pattern piece in placement order for ease of application. Examine the pattern and decide what part of the pattern is farthest from the eye? Do not think about the sky/ground right now; those are the background pieces that will be prepared later. Just look at the basic subject and surroundings. Is there a portion of a tree that shows from behind the building? Is the inside of the windows actually the farthest from the eye? Start with that piece and number it "1."

2 Which piece comes next? It might be the actual building front, followed by the framing around the window. Look at the pattern of the Point Loma Lighthouse and see how the numbering system works.

Lighthouse pattern with all pieces numbered in placement order.

CHAPTER 3

CONSTRUCTING THE BLOCK

In this chapter, you will learn to construct the block using your numbered pattern pieces. This is the fun part — you will see the block come to life with color and texture!

trace the numbered pieces

For the projects in this book, you will be using freezer paper, also called butcher paper, to trace the individual pattern pieces. Freezer paper is a white paper with one waxy side and one plain side. You will trace the pattern pieces on the paper side, then iron the waxy side to the fabric. Freezer paper is available in rolls, found at most grocery stores, and in 8½" x 11" sheets at some quilt shops (see Resources on page 126).

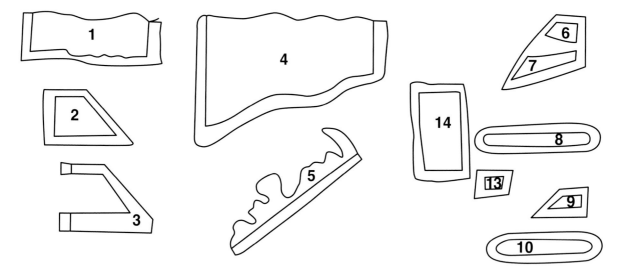

Extra outside lines on the traced piece indicate that more fabric is needed there to allow the next piece to adhere.

1 Place your pattern on a firm surface. Cover it with a piece of freezer paper as large as, or larger than, the pattern.

2 Trace piece number one.

3 Examine piece number one to determine where piece number two will overlap it. Draw an extra line about ⅛" outside the traced line of piece number one where the pieces will overlap. This will allow piece number two to adhere to piece number one when you assemble the quilt.

4 Continue to trace all of your pieces onto the freezer paper individually, one by one, numbering them as on the pattern. *Note:* After you trace each piece, examine the pattern to determine where the next piece would overlap the previous piece and draw extra ⅛" outlines where you see overlap.

5 Rough cut all individual pieces and place them on the fabric you selected for that piece. *Note:* Rough cutting means that you will not cut right on the lines, but just outside the lines. You will not cut right on the lines until after you add the fusible web and you are ready to actually build the block.

white for house

blue window reflection

brown tree trunk

sparkly net for light tower

black roof shadows

dark for tower and door

green bushes

green grass

green tree

stripe for picket fence

flowers

gray for shadows

dark gray for roof

Fabrics used for the lighthouse block.

tip...
Write the fabric color that you want to use for each piece right on the paper. When you cut out your freezer paper pattern pieces, it will be easy to organize by fabric color!

prepare the fabric pieces for fusible web

The purpose of placing the freezer paper template on the right side of the fabric is twofold. First, you can place the template right where you want it to take advantage of the print or texture on the fabric, or a lighter or darker area that best suits the look you want for that piece. Second, you do not have to trace pattern pieces from the reverse side of the pattern to keep everything facing the right direction. Your freezer paper template is right in front of you with the number in plain view. This is so much easier to work with while composing the block.

Typical fusible web package.

1 After all pieces are distributed to the proper fabric, take one fabric at a time to the ironing surface (with its pattern pieces).

2 Place the pattern pieces waxy-side down on the *right side* of the fabric, leaving a small space around each piece.

3 Iron the pattern pieces in place on the fabric using an iron set at hot.

4 Rough cut each piece individually to prepare for the addition of fusible web.

5 Cut a piece of fusible web a little larger than the pieces to be ironed onto it. Remove the protective paper on one side of the fusible web. *Note:* You can fit as many pattern pieces as manageable onto the fusible web. You will cut them out individually later.

6 Place your fabric pattern pieces on the fusible web. Place as many pieces as you can onto the fusible web, arranging them to fit the space available. Replace the protective paper on top of the pattern pieces; iron according to the manufacturer's directions. Leave the protective paper on the back.

7 Rough cut each of the pattern pieces individually. Place them aside where they will be ready for placement on the appliqué pressing sheet. You now have a group of pieces ready to go. They have the freezer paper on the *right side* of the fabric and the fusible web on the *wrong side*.

tips...

Some fusible web has protective paper on one side only. If this is the case for your fusible of choice, just place the pieces down on the fusible web and place the appliqué pressing sheet on top to protect your iron and ironing board. The fusible residue that may be left behind when you remove the pressing sheet can easily be wiped off with a paper towel.

If your pattern is too large to fit on the ironing board, use a table or other surface that is large enough to hold the entire pattern. Place several large towels or a folded blanket on the table, covered with a sheet. Iron them until they lay flat and straight. Use this for your ironing surface so you will not have to move the pattern to build the block.

When you have a piece that has a window in it, cut the window out first. As always, when you cut, hold your scissors fairly straight and move the fabric with the other hand. This will make a smoother line, especially when cutting curves. Move the fabric into the curve, not the scissors!

When you iron, just place the iron down on the pieces and hold in place for several seconds. Lift the iron, move to another place and press again. Use this up-and-down motion to avoid having the pieces shift out of position.

assemble the block

1 Clear your ironing surface.

2 Place your original pattern on the ironing surface.

3 Place the appliqué pressing sheet on top of the pattern; the pressing sheet is clear enough for you to see the pattern. Pin in place using straight pins in the top corners of the pattern and pressing sheet (the pins will not damage the pressing sheet).

4 Cut piece number one on the tracing lines.

5 Peel away the freezer paper from the front of the fabric. Peel away the protective paper from the back of the fabric; leaving the fusible glue that has been absorbed into the fabric.

6 Apply this piece on top of the appliqué pressing sheet using the pattern underneath as a guide. Press in place with your fingers. *Note:* Do not iron yet. It is best to apply several pieces before you iron; this allows you to be certain that you have them in the right place and that they overlap properly. If you have misnumbered a piece, pick it back up and put another one before it. You can also just lift an edge of a piece to slide the edge of another piece underneath.

7 After finger pressing several pieces, iron them directly to each other and to the pressing sheet.

8 Continue finger pressing and ironing until all of the pieces have been applied to the pressing sheet. Let it cool to the touch.

This house is completely fused and is ready for the next step.

borders

For appliqué work, it is a general rule to complete the appliqué on the oversized main block, trim to size *after* the appliqué is complete, and *then* add the borders. The reason for this is because hand appliqué work may cause some shrinking of the size of the block during the process of hand stitching. I have found, however, that in the case of machine appliqué on fusible web, the machine appliqué does not cause the block to shrink at all, therefore "trimming to size" is not needed. For the projects in this book, you should add all the borders as you prepare your background fabric. Borders should be added sides first, then top and bottom. In the projects, the cutting instructions list the specific border measurements for the quilt pictured. For alternative border options, see the instructions below. It can be fun to vary your borders from the ones shown, so use your imagination, creativity and color choices to border your pictoral block any way you desire!

Square Corner Borders

1 Measure the quilt top from top to bottom through the center. Cut two strips this length (using your desired width plus seam allowance).

2 Mark the midpoint of each strip and the midpoint of the sides of the quilt top.

3 Pin the strips to the sides of the quilt top, right sides together, matching the midpoints.

4 Sew the strips to the quilt top; press the seam allowance toward the border.

5 Measure the quilt top from side to side through the center. This measurement includes the added side borders. Cut two strips this length (using your desired width plus seam allowance).

6 Mark the midpoint of the strips and the midpoint of the top and bottom edges of the quilt top.

7 Pin the border strips to the top and bottom of the quilt top, right sides together, matching the midpoints.

8 Sew the strips to the quilt top; press the seam allowance toward the border.

Mitered Corner Borders

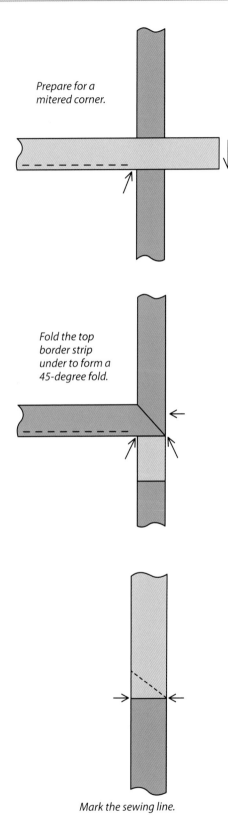

Prepare for a mitered corner.

Fold the top border strip under to form a 45-degree fold.

Mark the sewing line.

1 Measure the quilt top from side to side through the center. To that measurement, add two times the width of the border strip plus 5". For example, if the quilt top is 35" wide, and the border strips are 4" wide, you will need border strips that are 48" long (35" + 4" + 4" + 5" = 48"). Cut two strips this length.

2 Mark the midpoint of each strip and the midpoint of the top and bottom of the quilt top.

3 Pin the strips to the top and bottom of the quilt top, right sides together, matching these midpoints.

4 Sew the strips to the quilt top, starting ¼" from the edge and stopping ¼" before the opposite edge. The excess length will extend beyond each edge. Press these seams toward the border.

5 Measure the quilt top from top to bottom through the center. This measurement includes the added side borders. As in Step 1, add two times the width of the border strip plus 5". Cut two strips this length.

6 Mark the midpoint of the strips and the midpoint of the side edges of the quilt top.

7 Sew the strips to the quilt top, starting ¼" from the edge and stopptin ¼" before the opposite edge. Backstitch at the ¼" points to reinforce the edges and keep them from separating.

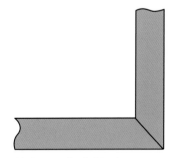

Make sure the finished corner lays flat.

8 To prepare for the miter, lay one corner of the quilt top on your ironing surface right side up. Open and press one border strip, then the adjacent one, laying it on top of the first strip.

9 Fold the top border strip under so that it meets the edge of the bottom border and forms a 45-degree angle.

10 Press this fold in place, then pin in place. Place your 90-degree ruler (square up the ruler or use a regular square ruler) over the corner to check that it is flat and square.

11 Fold the top bordered edge diagonally over the adjacent edge, right sides together. Align the long edges of the border strips together. Place your ruler along the folded edge of the quilt top to extend beyond the corner. Using a sharp pencil, draw a diagonal line across the border. This will be your sewing line.

12 Beginning at the inside corner, backstitch and sew on the line toward the outside point, being careful not to stretch. Backstitch at the end.

13 Turn the top over, checking to be sure the corner lays flat. Trim off the excess border fabric to the ¼" seam allowance. Press this seam open. Repeat for the remaining corners.

As an option for those of you who are miter-impaired, here is a neat way to accomplish the same thing. This also works well when working with pieced borders, border print fabrics or stripes.

1 Once you have the border strip folded under and aligned with the adjacent strip as shown at left in Step 11, press and pin firmly in place.

2 Using either a hand appliqué stitch or blind hem stitch on the machine with monofilament thread, stitch the diagonal fold down to the bottom strip.

3 Trim excess border fabric on the back to a ¼" seam allowance.

CHAPTER 4
FINISHING THE BLOCK

This chapter explains how to finish your quilt. From machine appliqué to preparing the batting and backing, you will learn what it takes to prepare your block for quilting.

machine appliqué

To machine appliqué, you will first need to start with the right materials: stabilizer, threads and needles. Once you have chosen these for your quilt, you can decide which machine-appliqué techniques will highlight the details in your quilt. Satin stitching is very attractive and accents the block nicely. Decorative stitches can enhance certain parts of the piece such as trees, bushes, flowers and grassy fields.

Stabilizer

A stabilizer keeps the piece flat and even as you sew. When satin stitching, stabilizers are very important because a close zigzag stitch causes the fabric to tunnel and pull toward the center of the zigzag. The stabilizer prevents this from happening.

There are many varieties of stabilizers on the market: tear-away, iron-on, water-soluble, etc. I prefer tear-away stabilizer, which can be removed after the appliqué is completed and before layering and quilting. Look for stabilizers in the notions section of your quilt shop.

Stabilizers are available in a variety of styles, from tear-away to water-soluble. Choose the type of stabilizer that works best for you and your quilt.

Threads

All of the fused pieces need to be stitched onto the block. To do this, you can choose the thread type you like to work with the most. Cotton threads in the same color as the piece you are sewing around will blend in with the piece. Embroidery threads give the piece a sheen, and can be the same color as the piece, or a little darker for emphasis. Metallic threads give a sparkle that highlights the entire block with its reflective character. You can even use monofilament thread when you want the stitching to be almost invisible. (See Resources on page 126.)

Needles

A variety of sewing machine needles are required according to the thread you have chosen for your block.

When using clear monofilament thread (for light-colored fabrics) or smoke color (for dark-colored fabrics), use a small needle, like size 60/8. This is the smallest needle size and can be obtained from your sewing machine shop and some quilt shops. The advantage of this needle is that the eye is very small and the needle is very thin. When you sew with this needle, the hole punched by it will also be very small. Since the thread is nearly invisible, you want to have the hole practically invisible as well.

For metallic threads, I recommend using topstitch 130N 100/16 needles. They are strong enough to penetrate multiple layers of fabric and fusible without breaking either the needle or the metallic thread. They have a larger, Teflon-lined eye and a groove in the back to allow the thread to slide through the eye without much drag. Metallic threads will sometimes shred and break if your tension is too tight or if you use a regular needle. When sewing with metallic threads, use monofilament thread in the bobbin and reduce the top tension slightly. Before sewing on your block, test the tension on a piece of scrap fabric.

You can use embroidery threads without fear of shredding or breaking. Use a monofilament thread or regular lingerie thread in the bobbin. A topstitch sharp needle works best for this type of thread.

Appliqué with four different threads. From the top: monofilament thread, embroidery (rayon) thread, metallic thread, cotton thread.

Satin Stitching

Satin stitching works well as an outline for appliqué pieces. Practice satin stitching using the same fabric you are using for your block. First, back the piece of fabric with stabilizer. Then, practice satin stitching in rows. Use varying widths and lengths, writing the setting numbers on the fabric next to each row. When you begin to stitch on your actual quilt block, you can use this handy reference to choose the type of satin stitch that will work best.

1 Cut a piece of tear-away stabilizer a little larger than your block. Place it on the back of the block. Pin in place at the four corners or use spray adhesive to hold it in place. *Note:* If using pins, remove the pins after sewing.

2 Use an open toe foot for machine appliqué (it allows you to see the piece you are sewing on clearly; it will probably have a red line at the inside center to use as a guide). Position the edge of your piece to be sewn just to the right of the guide mark; this way the outside part of the zigzag is just over the edge of the piece. If you use the guide mark, your satin stitch will be half on the fabric and half over the edge onto the background. Try both methods on a scrap piece to see which method you prefer.

3 Begin sewing. If you feel you are veering off the sewing line and not making a straight stitch, stop immediately. Remove the errant stitches and start again where you stopped.

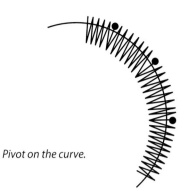

Pivot on the curve.

Sew a straight stitch to create the illusion of straight satin stitching.

Once you have completed the piece and find that some areas are a little off-line, sew a straight stitch very close to the edge of the satin stitching to give the illusion of a perfectly straight satin stitch.

When sewing around curves, always stop with your needle down on the outside of the curve. Raise the presser foot, pivot to position, lower the presser foot and continue.

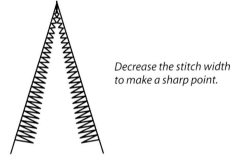

Decrease the stitch width to make a sharp point.

Turn corners while satin stitching.

Pivot the corner.

When satin stitching a diagonal point, such as a star point, reduce the width of the stitch by steps as you approach the point, stopping at the point with the needle down. Pivot to the other edge. Continue sewing, increasing the width to the starting width by steps as you sew.

On corners, sew to the corner, stopping with needle down at the outside edge of the corner. Raise the presser foot; pivot the fabric to a 45-degree angle.

When you stop sewing a line and cut your thread, the best way to avoid those little threads that pop up on the front is to take them to the back of the piece and knot them before cutting. Use a self-threading needle (or a needle with a large eye), thread the top thread onto the needle, and bring it to the back. Tie the bobbin thread and top thread in a knot and cut.

CHAPTER 5

FINISHING AND EMBELLISHING

Once your machine appliqué is completed on your block(s) and the borders have been added, it is time to quilt!

layering

1 Cut the batting 2" larger all around than the size of the block.

2 Cut the backing fabric this size, also.

3 Layer the batting, backing and quilt top, following one of the options below.

Option 1: Basting

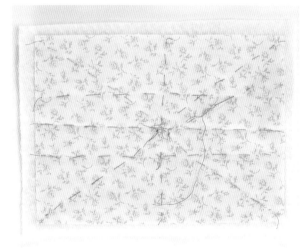

Baste the quilt top using a needle and thread.

1 Tape the backing fabric wrong-side up on a large table or the floor. Place the batting on top of the backing, smoothing it out with your hands. Place the block on top, right-side up, also smoothing it out. Tape or clip the top in place.

2 Using a long needle threaded with a single thread, stitch with large stitches down through the center from top to bottom, and again from side to side. Starting about 1" away from the basted line, baste again top to bottom on both sides of the first stitching line, and side to side on both sides of the first side-to-side stitching line. Continue stitching until the quilt top is completely basted.

3 Remove the tape or clips.

Option 2: Pinning

1 Tape the backing fabric wrong-side up on a large table or the floor. Place the batting on top of the backing, smoothing it out with your hands. Place the block on top, right-side up, also smoothing it out. Tape or clip the top in place.

2 Using small safety pins, pin the layers together, starting in the center of the top. Pin about every 2" on the top.

tip...
Using a grapefruit spoon with little ridges helps save your fingers when pinning. Also, some quilt shops have special tools to help with the pinning.

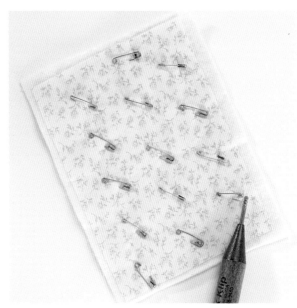

Baste the quilt top with small safety pins.

Option 3: Basting Spray

Note: The use of basting spray is ideal for free-motion quilting since there are no threads to catch on the presser foot and no pins to accidentally run over.

1 Tape the backing fabric wrong-side up on a large table or the floor. Place the batting on top of the backing, smoothing it with your hands.

2 Fold the batting in half, bringing the top edge to the bottom edge.

3 Using a basting spray, spray the folded batting lightly.

4 Fold the batting upward toward the top of the quilt back, smoothing carefully with your hands to ensure there are no tucks.

5 Fold the bottom of the batting upward toward the top.

6 Spray the folded batting lightly.

7 Unfold the batting back to the bottom, smoothing as you go.

Use basting spray to hold the quilt sandwich together.

8 Spray the entire top of the batting.

9 Carefully place the quilt top onto the sprayed batting, starting in the center.

10 Fold the quilt top in half top to bottom, placing it on the batting, smoothing as you go.

quilting

Once you have layered and basted your quilt top, you are ready to quilt. You can use a walking foot to sew around all the buildings and other subjects to let them pop out. Or, you can free-motion sew.

Straight Line Quilting

To prepare for straight line quilting, you simply need a special presser foot called a walking foot. This foot has a feature that "walks" with the movement of the foot to gently pull the top fabric through the machine at the same time the feed dogs are gently pulling the bottom fabric. This allows you to have a smooth quilting line. Without the walking foot, you can experience some tucks in the quilting process because of the thickness of the quilting "sandwich." *Note:* Some machines such as Pfaff have a built-in walking foot that requires no attachment. In the Pfaff machine, it is called the Independent Dual Feed. You can use it for most of your sewing, only disabling it when doing free-motion quilting.

Straight line quilting can be done in any pattern that you prefer. Many quilts benefit from grid quilting, which can be done with equally-spaced horizontal and vertical lines. A more pleasant look is the grid method using equally spaced diagonal lines creating a diamond pattern.

Many quilters like to "stitch in the ditch." This means that you stitch directly on seam lines, which is useful in pieced work, but not for appliqué work. When stitching in the ditch, it is important to stitch right in the seam, not just close to it and not just nearby!

Another straight line quilting favorite is to stitch ¼" away from seam lines on both sides of the seam. Hand quilters often use this technique. It gives you consistent stitching throughout your quilt, not heavy in some places and light in others. The consistency of the stitching is important for your quilt to lay flat.

Walking foot sewing limits you to fairly straight lines and makes it difficult to follow curves. If your quilt has a lot of straight lines, use your walking foot to stitch all the straight lines around your buildings, rooflines, etc. Then, free-motion quilt the sky and grass.

tip...
Stitch along seam lines with a wavy line that gives the piece some action. With this technique, you are not restricted to stitch right in the ditch!

Free-Motion Quilting

To prepare for free-motion quilting, you need a free-motion foot for your machine. Most machines have their own for purchase, or you may use a generic free-motion foot that fits many machines.

Free-motion quilting is the best method for machine quilting a fused pictorial appliqué piece. Due to the use of fusible web, it is difficult to hand quilt on these type of quilts.

Since these quilts require a lot of machine appliqué, you will not want to quilt heavily on an appliqué piece. To do so would require quilting overtop of the machine appliqué. Generally, quilting around buildings, trees and other objects is sufficient to bring out those shapes without disturbing the machine appliqué you worked so hard to make stand out. Lightly quilting on the sky and grass, ground or water areas in pleasing lines will fill out the quilting in a consistent manner. You can follow the lines of the clouds in a sky piece, or the wavy lines in the water. More opportunity for free-motion quilting is available in the borders.

It is a good idea to start with the buildings or other objects that make up the main portion of the block first, then go on to the sky, ground or water. After that it is prudent to stitch in the ditch where the border seam is located to stabilize the border edge. Stitch in the ditch where the second border is attached if you have one. The outer border is usually wider than the framing border, so you will have an opportunity to do some free-motion quilting there.

If you are new to free-motion quilting, here's a hint for practicing. Buy a pillow panel fabric, available at most fabric and craft stores. They are intended as sort of a picture for a pillow top and have objects on them you can follow to practice quilting. One that comes to mind is a picture in color of two bass fish jumping from a lake. It's fun to practice quilting scales on the fish and highlighting the seaweed!

Free-motion quilting gives you lots of leeway in your quilting. You can follow the lines of trees, bushes, buildings, clouds, water, etc. Try to keep your quilting consistent throughout the piece. If you quilt heavily in one area and not heavily in another area, you might have trouble keeping the quilt flat. The pictorial appliqué blocks do not require heavy quilting.

binding

To prepare the edges for the binding, use a long ruler and a large square-up ruler to trim the edges. Starting at one corner, check for squareness with the large square and trim the corner edges. Repeat for the other corners. Trim the sides keeping the border width accurate and lined up with the corner cuts. Double check the squareness by folding the quilt in half one way then the other to see that all the widths are the same.

If the edges are loose (perhaps the top was quilted loosely and not close to the edges), baste the edges together by machine using a walking foot. Make sure you are not stretching the edge as you sew about ⅛" from the edge to stabilize it.

When we think of binding, we often think it must be bias binding. When making a wallhanging, you can also cut binding on the straight of grain. This is because as it hangs, the straight-of-grain binding will not stretch out as bias would. Bias was used on bed quilts to keep wear to a minimum.

1 Measure around the edges of the wallhanging. Add these measurements plus 10" to give you extra for mitering the corners and to join the binding.

2 Cut the binding strips 2½" wide, joining them as shown below to achieve the length you need as in the previous step.

3 Join the strips with a 45-degree angle joint; it has less bulk and you will not have a bump in the middle of the binding.

4 Press the binding in half lengthwise, making sure you press the seams open. Set it aside until you make your sleeve or rod pocket.

Sleeve

1 Measure the width of the quilt. Cut (or piece) a strip that is 9" by the quilt width measurement.

2 Turn under the outside edges; topstitch a ¼" hem.

3 Press this sleeve strip in half lengthwise, **wrong** sides together.

4 Open the sleeve and fold one long side toward the center press line. Press the fold, then sew as close to the folded edge as possible along the long edge.

5 Repeat Step 4 on the other side, folding that edge toward the center, pressing and sewing close to the folded edge.

6 Again, folding the sleeve in half lengthwise (your first pressing line is still there), stitch a ¼" seam making a tube with the **right** side out. Press the seam open.

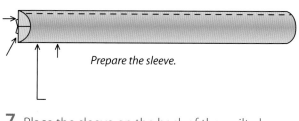

Prepare the sleeve.

7 Place the sleeve on the back of the quilt along the top raw edge, centering it between the outside edges, with the pressed seam facing the quilt top. Pin in place.

Binding Continued

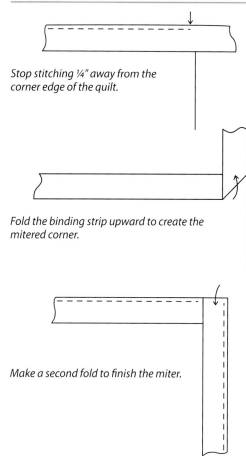

Stop stitching ¼" away from the corner edge of the quilt.

Fold the binding strip upward to create the mitered corner.

Make a second fold to finish the miter.

1 Back to the binding strip! Sew the binding strip to the quilt edges on the front of the quilt, leaving about 5" loose before you start stitching; this will be the joining area at the end. Sew with a ¼" seam. *Note:* As you sew, you are catching the sleeve top in the seam.

2 Miter the corners: Stop stitching ¼" from the corner of the quilt top with your needle down. Turn the top at a 45-degree angle and stitch to the outside corner.

3 Stop and cut the threads.

4 Fold the strip straight up toward the side you just stitched, then refold it toward the new edge to be stitched. Line up the second fold with the outer edge of the quilt. Line up the raw edges of the binding with the raw edges of the quilt.

5 Continue sewing the binding to the quilt, starting at the outer edge and sewing through all layers at the corner. Repeat the miter at each corner as described.

6 Stop sewing about 16" before the place where you started sewing; this will give you plenty of room to join the binding edges.

7 Position the loose binding along the quilt edge until the ends meet. Fold each back and press, making a fold line on each. Cut the ends off ¼" from the fold line.

8 Open the strips, place them right sides together. Stitch them together. Finger press the seam open.

Refold the binding strip wrong sides together, and place them on the quilt top, aligning the raw edges. Finish the seam.

9 Wrap the binding around to the back of the quilt; place the folded edge of the binding on top of the stitching line. Blind stitch by hand.

10 When you reach the corner, the miter is already folded for you on the front. On the back, fold one side down, then the other, creating a nice miter. The fold should be opposite the one on the front side to distribute the bulk evenly for both sides. This will make a nice, flat corner. Blind stitch the mitered folds.

Sleeve Continued

1 Back to the sleeve! You have attached the sleeve to the quilt top as you stitched on the binding. Now, pin the bottom of the sleeve to the quilt top. You will notice that the back of the sleeve, the part that has the seam, will lay flat on the quilt, but the front of the sleeve is a little puffy. This is correct. This will allow you to put a rod through the sleeve easily, and the shape of the rod will not show on the front of the quilt.

2 Hand stitch the sleeve back to the quilt, including the side edges so that the rod will not accidentally go into the part between the sleeve and the quilt.

PROJECTS

These projects are designed to encourage your own creativity, and each one has a different technique or embellishment idea to spark your interest. The patterns have been created for you and are provided in the back of the book. When in doubt about a step in the process, refer to Chapters 1-4 for a refresher on the basic assembly instructions.

Note: For each project, I give specific cutting measurements for the borders. Since everyone's ¼" seam can vary widely, I recommend that you measure your own block before cutting border strips to ensure your border strips will fit your block.

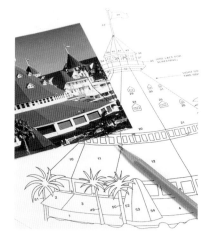

BASIC SUPPLIES FOR ALL PROJECTS...

- Pencil, pen or fine-point marker

- Freezer paper (sometimes called butcher paper or appliqué template paper)

- Fusible web

- Appliqué pressing sheet

- Tear-away stabilizer

- Scissors for paper

- Scissors for fabric

- Iron and mat (or other ironing surface)

- Long-handled tweezers

- Pins (glass-head pins work best and will not melt under the heat of the iron)

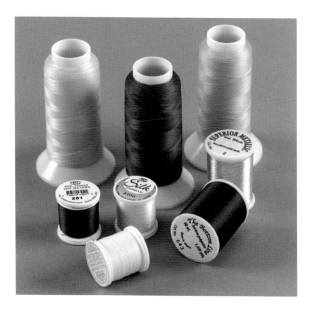

- Threads for appliqué (embroidery, metallic and cotton in colors that coordinate with your fabrics, and clear monofilament thread)

- Sewing machine

- Bobbins threaded in neutral color (you can thread the bobbin with the same color thread you will be using on the top)

the golden gate bridge

San Francisco, California

The Golden Gate Bridge is a spectacular landmark recognized all over the world. Creating this block with realism is a small challenge, partially achieved by using organdy as the ever-present fog. The vertical cables and horizontal suspension cable are also an important aspect of the bridge and can be accentuated with heavy stitching and couching. The bridge extends beyond the borders for a striking perspective. This pattern, however, is one of the simplest due to the fact that there are only a limited number of pieces. For an added touch, you could put one or several little sailboats in the bay.

FABRICS

- Fat quarter of blue hand-dyed or commercial sky fabric for the sky
- Fat quarter of gray-green for the background hills
- Fat quarter of blue for the water
- Fat eighth of mottled orange fabric for the bridge
- Fat eighth of gray for the road
- Scrap of white for the small sailboat
- ¼ yd. white organdy for the fog
- ⅛ yd. luminescent organdy for the top fog
- Fat eighth of black for the framing border
- Fat eighth of white-on-white for the second border
- Fat quarter of green for the third border

blue sky

rippling water

mottled gray roadway

orange bridge

distant hills

white sailboat

CUTTING INSTRUCTIONS

From the sky fabric, cut:
- One 5" x 15½" rectangle

From the background hill fabric, cut:
- One 1½" x 15½" rectangle

From water fabric, cut:
- One 5" x 15½" rectangle

From the bridge fabric, cut:
- According to pattern

From the road fabric, cut:
- According to pattern

From the small sailboat fabric, cut:
- According to pattern

From the white organdy fog fabric, cut:
- One 1½" x 13" rectangle
- One 1½" x 12" rectangle

From the luminescent organdy fog fabric, cut:
- One 1½" x 10" rectangle

From the black framing border fabric, cut:
- Two 1½" x 9½" side strips
- Two 1½" x 15½" top and bottom border strips

From the white second border fabric, cut:
- Two 2" x 11½" side border strips
- Two 2" x 16" top and bottom border strips

From the green third border fabric, cut:
- Two 2½" x 11½" side border strips
- Two 2½" x 19½" top and bottom border strips

Choosing Fabric

When selecting the fabric for the bridge, avoid solid orange. It would appear flat and uninteresting. Choose a mottled orange, perhaps a batik or hand-dyed fabric that has some texture. The roadway is a paved road, so dark gray, also textured, will provide the realistic look.

You may want to be daring and choose fabric entirely different than shown here. One student I worked with chose a twilight sky with metallic bits in it, and a dark water fabric. She appliquéd the bridge and cabling with metallic threads for sparkle and added beads for the lighting. It turned out beautifully!

tip...

To give the bridge the prominence it commands, bring it out into the framing (or border) of the block to give it a three-dimensional look. Add the borders before starting the machine appliqué.

Prepare the Background Fabric

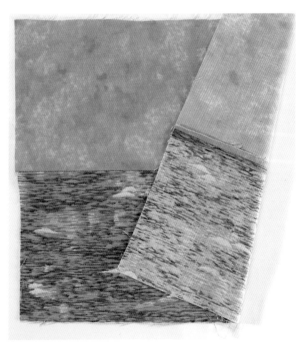

Prepare the background.

1 Sew the sky and water fabric together with a ¼" seam. Press the seam open for less bulk. *Note:* When you place the distant hills on the background later, it will cover the seam.

2 Sew the side borders to the sky and water background panel. Press the seam toward the border.

3 Sew the top and bottom borders to the sky and water background panel. Press the seam toward the border.

4 Set the background aside until after you have built the block on the pressing sheet.

Trace the Pieces and Build the Block

Follow the instructions in Chapter 3 to trace the pieces and assemble the block.

Machine Appliqué

Note: Use an open toe presser foot for machine appliqué. You can use a neutral-color bobbin thread or one to match your top thread.

1 Place a piece of tear-away stabilizer underneath the block; this will keep the stitching flat and smooth and will keep the satin stitches from "tunneling" the fabric.

2 Using the appropriate color thread, outline the distant hills. Blanket stitch on top of the hills to add texture.

3 Using blue thread, blanket stitch the bottom of the hills to the water.

4 Using orange thread, satin stitch the stanchions and the outside span next to the roadway.

Add the Suspension Cables and Supporting Wires

1 Place the pattern on a light box or window, taping to keep it steady. Place your block on top.

2 Trace the suspension cables and supporting wires on the far side of the bridge using a pencil, chalk pencil or water-erasable pen.

tip...

Satin stitching makes a beautiful outline for the bridge. When starting the satin stitch, practice on a scrap piece with the stabilizer on the back to get the feel of it before you stitch on your block. Look for general hints for satin and decorative stitching on page 36.

Satin stitch on the bridge.

MAKE THE SUPPORTING WIRES LOOK REALISTIC

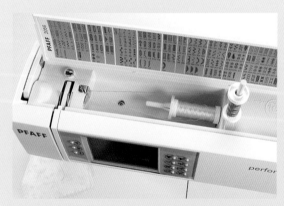

Create a custom color by threading your machine with two threads.

To create a custom color for the supporting wires, try stitching with two different color threads through the same needle. Use a topstitch or embroidery needle, size #90 or #100. These have larger eyes and will accommodate two threads. If your sewing machine does not have two spool pins, you can easily adapt it to use two spools on one pin. Cut 5"-6" of a plastic straw and place it on the spool pin. The pin will be extended enough to hold two spools of thread. Pull the threads from the spools in opposite directions to avoid tangling. Thread the two as one except at the tension discs where one thread should be placed on each side of the disc. Use this technique to blend the colors, or to add a sparkle by selecting a metallic as one of the thread choices.

If your machine has a triple stitch feature, also called the reinforced stitch, this will make the supporting wires look thicker and show more of both colors of thread. The triple stitch does one stitch forward, one back, one forward, then goes forward again, back, forward, etc. If you do not have this feature, you can sew over the lines twice using a straight stitch to make them look thicker.

3 Sew the supporting wires by starting at the far side of the block. Sew up to the top cable, pivot and take a few stitches on the top cable line, pivot again and sew down to the bridge, pivot, sew across the bridge to the next line, pivot, sew up to the top cable line, and so on. *Note:* Notice that as you come forward, the wires are farther apart. This gives the illusion of distance. The supporting wires extend beyond the side border.

4 Once the far side supporting wires are completed, remove the two threads and rethread the machine with monofilament thread or orange thread.

5 Cut three strands of orange embroidery floss 18" long. Knot one end of three strands. Thread the floss into a large-eye hand-sewing needle. Bring the floss up from the back of the fabric to the front at the top of the far side stanchion. Once the floss is on the front in position, remove the needle and place the block in the machine with your presser foot down over the floss.

6 Hold the floss over the traced suspension cable line. Using a couching foot or open toe foot and a small, narrow zigzag stitch, sew (couch) the floss across to the near stanchion, stop with needle down, pivot, and continue the couching out into the border. *Note:* Couching is simply placing some kind of thicker thread, yarn, pearl cotton or floss right over the area you want to cover, and attaching it with a small zigzag stitch with monofilament or other thread in your sewing machine.

7 Rethread the floss into a large eye needle again, and bring the floss to the back of the block. Turn the block over and knot the thread on the back.

8 Repeat Steps 1-7 for the near supporting wires.

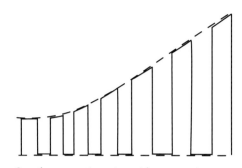

Sew the supporting wires without stopping.

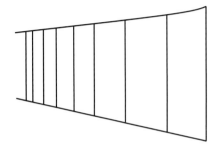

The wires are closer together in the distance.

Couch floss onto the quilt to make the suspension cables.

Add the Sailboat (optional)

1 Apply fusible web to the back of a small (3" x 3") piece of white fabric. Do not remove the protective paper from the fusible web.

2 Trace the sailboat onto the paper side of freezer paper.

3 Iron the tracing to the right side of the fabric.

4 Cut out the traced shape of the boat. Remove the freezer paper and the protective paper from the fusible web on the back of the piece.

5 Place the boat on the water where desired; iron in place.

6 Machine appliqué the boat with clear monofilament thread using a short, narrow zigzag stitch.

Add the Fog

1 Place the iridescent rectangle of fog on the block in whatever position you choose; pin in place at the corners.

2 Thread the machine with monofilament thread. Using a small, narrow zigzag stitch, sew around the fog in a shape that is reminiscent of fog, almost like the look of a cloud. Trim away the excess organdy with small appliqué scissors. Add more fog as desired.

Typical San Francisco fog on the bridge.

tip...
If you want the distant hills to appear paler, like you are seeing them through a mist, place a piece of white tulle over the area and sew in place with monofilament thread and a tiny zigzag stitch. Trim the excess tulle away. This will give it the look of a misty morning fog.

Finish the Quilt

1 Using a pair of long-handled tweezers, grab the stabilizer and tear it away. Hold the stitching line with your finger and thumb to keep it firm while you tear away the paper. This will avoid allowing the stitches to come loose.

2 Set this block aside if you are making a larger wallhanging quilt until you have all the blocks for the quilt completed. Or, finish it as a single wallhanging unit by layering it with batting and a backing, and following the quilting instructions on page 40. *Note:* This block does not lend itself to heavy quilting, just quilt outlining the bridge, and a little in the sky and water. You would not want to quilt over the fog or the cables.

Note: We are assuming that the bridge was closed the day we took the picture, therefore no traffic!

the old family barn

This is actually the barn that was on my family's property in Pennsylvania, where my uncle had a dairy farm. I can remember spending summers at the farm, helping with the chores, playing with the baby chicks and feeding the pigs. Unfortunately, the barn no longer exists. Looking at the old barn brings back many good memories for me. I am sure many of you have warm memories from your past, also!

FABRICS

- Fat quarter of blue for the sky
- Fat quarter of green for the grass
- Fat quarter of wood print for the buildings
- Fat eighth of stone print for the buildings
- Scraps for other parts
- Fat quarter of black for the framing border
- Fat quarter of red for the first border

red barn wood

silo (dark)

dark barn wood

dark areas

dark windows/doorways

tree trunk

stones

grass

silo (light)

roof

silo (top rim)

sky

CUTTING INSTRUCTIONS

From the sky fabric, cut:
- One 15½" x 12¾" rectangle

From the grass fabric, cut:
- One 15½" x 4" rectangle

From the wood and stone fabrics, cut:
- According to pattern

From the scraps, cut:
- According to pattern

From the black framing border fabric, cut:
(Note: Attach fusible web to the back before cutting.)
- Two 2½" x 9½" side border strips
- Two 2½" x 12¼" top and bottom border strips

From the red first border fabric, cut:
- Two 2½" x 12" side border strips
- Two 2½" x 19½" top and bottom border strips

Prepare the Background Fabric

1 Sew the sky and grass fabrics together with a ¼" seam. Press the seam open for less bulk. *Note:* When you place the barn on the background later, it will cover the seam.

2 Trim the background to the size shown on the pattern.

3 Sew the red side border strips to the sides of the background fabric. Press the seams toward the borders.

4 Sew the red top and bottom border strips to the top and bottom of the background fabric. Press the seams toward the borders.

5 Set aside the black framing border strips until the machine appliqué is completed.

Trace the Pieces and Build the Block

Follow the instructions in Chapter 3 to trace the pieces and assemble the block.

tip...
Optional setting: Extend the building on the right side of the block past the thin framing border. The extension of the building is provided with the pattern. Add the framing border on top of the block to give the illusion that the building continues outside the border.

Machine Appliqué

Note: Use an open toe presser foot for machine appliqué. You can use a neutral-color bobbin thread or one to match your top thread.

1 Place a piece of tear-away stabilizer underneath the block; this will keep the stitching flat and smooth and will keep the satin stitches from "tunneling" the fabric.

2 Using the appropriate thread color, outline the pieces using satin stitch. Add further texture with blanket stitches.

3 Sew vines and weeds along the bottom of the buildings to add further realism to this old barn.

Thread "paint" vines and weeds along the edge of the barn.

Add the Framing Border

1 Place the black framing border strips in place and iron onto the block, referring to the photo of the completed quilt.

2 Machine appliqué the border in place using smoke color monofilament thread and a short, narrow zigzag stitch.

3 Add a piece of tree fabric over the framing border strips; machine appliqué in place.

Finish the Quilt

1 Using a pair of long-handled tweezers, grab the stabilizer and tear it away. To prevent the stitches from loosening as you tear away the stabilizer, hold the stitching line with your finger and thumb to keep it firm.

2 Set this block aside if you are making a larger wallhanging quilt until you have all the blocks for the quilt completed. Or, finish it as a single wallhanging unit by layering it with batting and a backing, and following the quilting instructions on page 40.

the alamo

San Antonio, Texas

Almost everyone recognizes The Alamo. It is the most popular tourist attraction in Texas. It was originally named Mission San Antonio de Valero. Visiting The Alamo for the first time, I was struck by its size. It is surrounded by high-rise buildings and it remains a small fortress in the middle of the city of San Antonio. But it continues to instill a sense of pride in all Texans and people who value freedom.

Photo of the Alamo.

FABRICS

- Fat quarter of blue for the sky

- Fat quarter of green for the grass

- Fat quarter of beige, tan or ecru for the Alamo building

- Scrap of dark fabric for the inside of the windows

- Fat quarter of dark green for the trees and leaves

- Fat quarter of beige, tan or ecru for the border

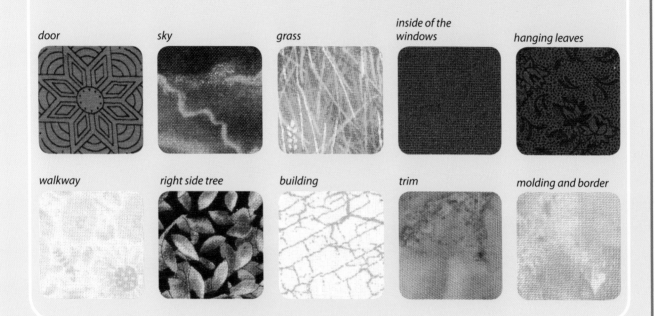

door *sky* *grass* *inside of the windows* *hanging leaves*

walkway *right side tree* *building* *trim* *molding and border*

CUTTING INSTRUCTIONS

From the sky fabric, cut:
- One 11½" x 8½" rectangle

From the grass fabric, cut:
- One 11½" x 2" strip

From the border fabric, cut:
- Two 3" x 13½" side border strips
- Two 3" x 15½" top and bottom border strips

From the building fabrics, cut:
- According to the pattern

Prepare the Background Fabric

A dramatic sky makes more impact on the block.

1 Sew the sky and grass fabric together with a ¼" seam. Press the seam open for less bulk.

2 Sew the side border strips to the sides of the background fabric. Press the seams toward the borders.

3 Sew the top and bottom border strips to the top and bottom of the background fabric. Press the seams toward the borders.

Trace the Pieces and Build the Block

Follow the instructions in Chapter 3 to trace the pieces and assemble the block.

Machine Appliqué

Note: Use an open toe presser foot for machine appliqué. You can use a neutral-color bobbin thread or one to match your top thread.

1 Place a piece of tear-away stabilizer underneath the block; this will keep the stitching flat and smooth and will keep the satin stitches from "tunneling" the fabric.

2 Using the appropriate thread color, outline the building and other details. Change top threads as you go from the building to the details around the door and windows.

Add Loose Leaves to the Tree on the Left

1 Iron fusible web to the wrong side of a scrap of dark green fabric.

2 When cool, peel the protective paper away from the fusible.

3 Place another scrap of the same dark green fabric on the back of the fused square, with the wrong side on the fusible. Press.

4 Using small scissors and a free-motion cutting curve, cut several leaves approximately ¼" x 1".

5 Trace the hanging branch lines from the pattern onto the block using a pencil, chalk pencil or water-soluble ink pen.

6 Using brown thread and a triple or reinforced stitch, sew the lines of the branches.

tip...

Use two threads in one needle for more color variance. See page 50 in the Golden Gate Bridge project for more details.

Cut leaves for the tree.

Sew the leaves onto the branches just at the tip so the leaves hang free.

Machine appliqué the block.

7 Using a straight stitch set at 2.0 or slightly shorter than the normal stitch length, sew starting at the edge of the block right on top of the previously sewn branch lines. Stop after about 6 or 8 stitches and lay down a leaf with one end touching the sewing line. Sew two stitches onto the leaf and, using your reverse stitch, go back to the branch. Continue on the branch a short distance and again apply another leaf. Continue with this procedure until you have added as many leaves as desired.

Finish the Quilt

1 Using a pair of long-handled tweezers, grab the stabilizer and tear it away. To prevent the stitches from loosening as you tear away the stabilizer, hold the stitching line with your finger and thumb to keep it firm.

2 Set this block aside if you are making a larger wallhanging quilt until you have all the blocks for the quilt completed. Or, finish it as a single wallhanging unit by layering it with batting and a backing, and following the quilting instructions on page 40.

killer whales at sea

Killer whales observed in a sea park astonish visitors because of their size as well as their intelligence. These mammals look like they were drawn and painted by a cartoonist and are a joy to watch. The beauty of the whales against the turquoise water, watching their leaps and interaction with the trainers is a grand adventure. But seeing them in their natural habitat at sea is an awesome sight to behold!

tip...

If you don't have a photo to use, get creative, as I did for this quilt. I drew the whales and made up an appropriate background.

FABRICS

Fat quarter of blue or ocean green for the ocean

Fat quarter of light blue for the sky

Fat eighths of three shades of medium to dark blue for the distant mountains

Fat eighth of black for the whales

Scraps of white for the whales (at least 6" x 6")

Scraps of netting or lace for the water splash (at least 8" x 8")

Fat quarter of white-on-white for the framing border

Fat quarter of medium to dark blue for the second border

Fat eighth of white or gray tulle (optional — see further instructions under the Machine Appliqué section)

CUTTING INSTRUCTIONS

From the ocean fabric, cut:
- One 10" x 9½" piece

From the sky fabric, cut:
- One 9" x 9½" piece

From the mountain fabric, cut:
- According to pattern

From the black scraps for the whales, cut:
- According to pattern

From the white scraps for the whales, cut:
- According to pattern

From the netting or lace, cut:
- One 2" x 3" rectangle

From the white-on-white framing border fabric, cut:
- Two 1½" x 14½" side border strips
- Two 1½" x 12" top and bottom border strips

From the blue second border fabric, cut:
- Two 3½" x 16" side border strips
- Two 3½" x 17" top and bottom border strips

Prepare the Background Fabric

1 Sew the sky and water fabric together with a ¼" seam. Press the seam open for less bulk.

2 Add fusible web to the already-cut mountain pieces.

3 Fuse the mountain pieces to the background according to the pattern.

4 Sew the framing border side strips to the sides of the background fabric. Press the seams toward the borders.

5 Sew the framing border top and bottom strips to the top and bottom of the background fabric. Press the seams toward the borders.

6 Sew the second border side strips to the sides of the panel. Press the seams outward.

7 Sew the second border top and bottom strips to the top and bottom of the panel. Press the seams outward.

Trace the Pieces and Build the Block

Follow the instructions in Chapter 3 to trace the pieces and assemble the block.

Machine Appliqué

Note: Use an open toe presser foot for machine appliqué. You can use a neutral-color bobbin thread or one to match your top thread.

1 Place a piece of tear-away stabilizer underneath the block; this will keep the stitching flat and smooth and will keep the satin stitches from "tunneling" the fabric.

2 To add more distance to the farthest mountain, cut a piece of tulle about 2" larger than the area you wish to cover. Place it roughly on top of the mountain. Machine appliqué the mountain's outline with monofilament thread with a short, narrow zigzag stitch. Trim away the excess tulle.

3 Using matching thread, machine appliqué the next mountain with a decorative or satin stitch.

4 Outline the white areas of the whales with white cotton thread or embroidery thread using a narrow satin stitch.

5 Outline the black areas of the whales with black cotton thread or embroidery thread using a narrow satin stitch. *Note:* Embroidery thread gives an accented shine to the whales.

Add the Water Splash

1 Freehand cut (or follow the pattern) the netting or lace for the water splash. Do not add fusible web.

2 Pin the netting or lace to the background where indicated on the pattern. Sew all around with monofilament thread.

3 Thread-paint more splash with white thread using free-motion style to give it a watery appearance.

Finish the Quilt

1 Using a pair of long-handled tweezers, grab the stabilizer and tear it away. To prevent the stitches from loosening as you tear away the stabilizer, hold the stitching line with your finger and thumb to keep it firm.

2 Set this block aside if you are making a larger wallhanging quilt until you have all the blocks for the quilt completed. Or, finish it as a single wallhanging unit by layering it with batting and a backing, following the instructions on page 38.

3 Quilt around the bodies of the whales with monofilament thread (use smoke-color monofilament so it will not be visible on dark fabric).

4 Use shiny metallic thread to quilt the water splash.

5 Quilt the water with wavy lines.

6 Quilt the background hills just as densely as the water to keep your block flat.

old ironside sailing ship

Tall ships are magnificent reminders of the past and project a romantic image in our minds of the glorious days when they sailed the oceans with dignity and grace. The romance of the past can come to life in the block when you give it a three-dimensional effect by attaching some of the sails just at the corners, leaving them loose as the actual billowing sails appear when these tall ships are underway.

Photo of a ship used in composite with others to create this quilt.

FABRICS

- Fat quarter of blue for the sky
- Fat quarter of blue for the water
- Fat quarter of white for the sails
- Fat quarter of off-white for the shadowed sails
- Scraps of black and red for the ship
- Scraps of brown for the mast
- Fat quarter of black for the framing border
- Fat quarter of sky blue for the second border
- Hank of brown embroidery floss for the rigging
- Cheesecloth for the water splash on the bow (find this in the baking section of a grocery store or at a fabric shop)

blue sky

dark blue water

light sails

shadowed sails

hull

hull at waterline

floss for rigging

cheesecloth for water splash

CUTTING INSTRUCTIONS

From the sky fabric, cut:
- One 12½" x 11½" rectangle

From the water fabric, cut:
- One 4" x 11½" rectangle

From the white sail fabric, cut:
- According to pattern

From the off-white sail fabric, cut:
- According to pattern

From the black and red scraps for the ship, cut:
- According to pattern

From the brown scraps for the mast, cut:
- According to pattern

From the black framing border fabric, cut:
- Two 1½" x 14½" side border strips
- Two 1½" x 13" top and bottom border strips

From the sky blue second border fabric, cut:
- Two 3½" x 16½" side border strips
- Two 3¼" x 18¼" top and bottom border strips

Prepare the Background Fabric

1 Sew the sky and water fabric together with a 1/4" seam. Press the seam open for less bulk. *Note: The ship will partially cover the seam.*

2 Sew the framing border side strips to the sides of the background fabric. Press the seams toward the borders.

3 Sew the framing border top and bottom strips to the top and bottom of the background fabric. Press the seams toward the borders.

4 Sew the second border side strips to the sides of the panel. Press the seams outward.

5 Sew the second border top and bottom strips to the top and bottom of the panel. Press the seams outward.

Trace the Pieces and Build the Block

Follow the instructions in Chapter 3 to trace the pieces and assemble the block.

Machine Appliqué

Note: Use an open toe presser foot for machine appliqué.
You can use a neutral-color bobbin thread or one to match your top thread.

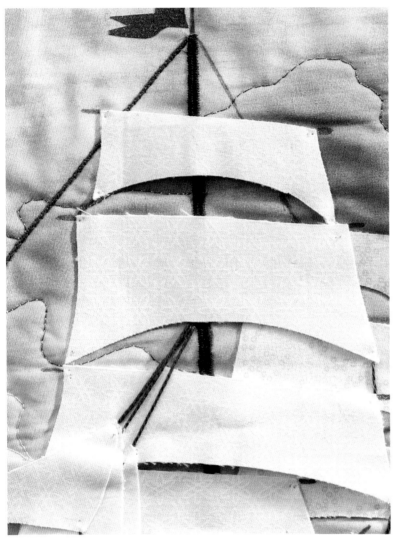

1 Place a piece of tear-away stabilizer underneath the block; this will keep the stitching flat and smooth and will keep the satin stitches from "tunneling" the fabric.

2 Using the appropriate thread color, outline the parts of the ship.

3 Satin stitch around all other pieces, including the fused-on sails. *Note:* Do not attach the loose sails until all other stitching is done.

4 Position the double-sided sails in place with a dot of glue on the corners; let dry.

5 Sew the sails down with a zigzag stitch on the corners only.

Tack the sails at the corners only.

Lettering

To add the ship's name, use one of the following methods:
- Neatly print the name with a permanent fabric ink pen.
- Print the name on printable fabric and sew it to the ship.
- Print the ship's name on paper, use carbon paper to trace over the letters, then embroider the letters using one or two strands of black embroidery floss.
- Print the name, use carbon paper to trace over the letters, then paint the letters on the ship using a small brush and fabric paint.

Add the Rigging

Note: Placing the rigging in position before quilting the block will cause a little problem when it's time to quilt; you will have to be extra careful not to snag or tangle the rigging. One option is to place the rigging on the block after the quilting is completed. This presents another set of problems, as the knots now appear on the back of the quilt! It's your choice on how you want to proceed.

1 Refer to the pattern for the rigging placement.

2 Thread a needle with three strands of brown embroidery floss. Knot one end, and come up from the back at one end of the rigging area. Place the floss across the ship to the other end of that rigging; stitch to the back and knot.

3 Repeat Steps 1 and 2 for each rigging area, remembering to knot before and after placing the floss in position.

Complete the rigging on the tall ship.

Add the Water Splash

1 Using a single layer of cheesecloth, freehand cut a piece approximately 2" wide by the length of the ship bottom.

2 Using your fingers, gently stretch and skew the cheesecloth into an irregular shape, being careful not to shred the cheesecloth.

3 Rub the glue stick on the bottom of the ship and on a little bit of the water around it. Place the cheesecloth on the glue, manipulating it until it looks like a water splash. Trim away the excess cheesecloth. Let dry.

4 Machine sew the cheesecloth to the block using monofilament thread and a short, narrow zigzag stitch. Sew around the edges and also sew several rows along the cheesecloth thread lines to secure it in place.

Use cheesecloth to create the illusion of a water splash.

Finish the Quilt

1 Using a pair of long-handled tweezers, grab the stabilizer and tear it away. To prevent the stitches from loosening as you tear away the stabilizer, hold the stitching line with your finger and thumb to keep it firm.

2 Set this block aside if you are making a larger wallhanging quilt until you have all the blocks for the quilt completed. Or, finish it as a single wallhanging unit by layering it with batting and a backing, and following the quilting instructions on page 40. *Note:* Obviously someone must have ordered the crew to abandon ship! There appears to be no one aboard!

sunset at lahaina

Maui, Hawaii

Photo of the sunset.

While attending the Old Lahaina Luau, billed as the only authentic Hawaiian luau in Hawaii (versus a Polynesian Luau), the sun began to set presenting me with a luscious photo opportunity! I immediately put down my Mai Tai, grabbed the camera and took several shots. One of them turned out so beautifully, I knew that I had to re-create it. The rendition is not difficult — finding a beautiful sunset sky fabric is the key!

FABRICS

- Fat quarter of dramatic sunset fabric, preferably hand dyed for the sky

- Scrap of blue for the water

- Fat quarter of solid black for the foreground

- Fat eighths of dark, medium and light green for the foliage

- ⅛ yd. dark Ultrasuede for the palm tree silhouettes

- Fat quarter of sunset colors for the framing border

- Fat quarter of black for the second border

yellow for torch fires

blue green for foliage

light green for foliage

medium green for foliage

medium dark for foliage

dark for foliage

black for background

black Ultrasuede for palm trees (fringe will not ravel)

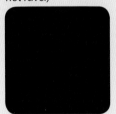

blue fabric with reflection for water

sky (hand-dyed fabric)

CUTTING INSTRUCTIONS

From the sky fabric, cut:
- One 9" x 14" piece

From the water fabric, cut:
- One 2½" x 14" piece

From the foreground fabric, cut:
- One 15½" x 14" piece

From the foliage fabric, cut:
- According to pattern

From the palm tree fabric, cut:
- According to pattern

For the sunset framing border fabric, cut:
- Two 1" x 20" side border strips
- Two 1" x 15" top and bottom border strips

For the black second border fabric, cut:
- Two 3" x 21½" side border strips
- Two 3" x 19" top and bottom border strips

Small block with one foliage fabric and one black piece for the palm fronds.

Actual quilt block using many shades of green for the foliage.

tip...

This photo was different than most of my other photo quilts because the foliage is in the foreground. Since it was highlighted by the flash from the camera, it showed several different values of green. To see how it would look using just one multicolored green fabric, I made a small block about 8½" x 11" first. After making the small block, I decided that in the larger version, many shades of green would do more justice to the foliage, and that the block seemed to call for individual palm fronds in lieu of just one silhouette. If you cannot decide how to choose fabrics for your block, it is helpful to audition fabrics by making a smaller version to give you an idea of just how it will look. If you like the result, move on to the full-size version with the fabric you chose. If you don't like the result, you have the opportunity to select other fabrics and try again.

ORGANIZE THE PATTERN PIECES

This pattern has a lot of numbered pieces for the foliage in the foreground. To help you get organized, refer to the original photo to decide which colors and shades you want for each area. On a piece of notepaper, write down the fabric choices in columns so you can list the pattern piece numbers required for each fabric in the proper column. Then, when you begin to trace your pattern pieces, trace each fabric group numbers on one piece of freezer paper. Place these tracings with that fabric ready to be ironed. Do the same with all fabrics.

Make a mental note of this procedure; it avoids confusion when you have many pieces for one color. To make it easier for you on this project, I am including this list for you.

Water fabric: 2, 3, 4, 5, 38, 60, 73, 74

Light green foliage fabric: 62, 63, 65, 66, 67, 68, 69, 71, 72

Medium green foliage fabric: 12, 13, 15, 20, 24, 25, 28, 31, 33, 41, 44, 50, 52, 53, 54, 55, 61, 64

Dark green foliage fabric: 6, 7, 8, 9, 10, 11, 14, 16, 17, 18, 19, 21, 22, 23, 26, 27, 29, 30, 32, 34, 35, 36, 37, 39, 40, 42, 43, 45, 46, 47, 48, 49, 51, 56, 57, 58, 59, 70

Palm tree fabric: 79, 80, 81, 82, 83, 84

Yellow flame fabric: 75, 76, 77, 78

Foreground fabric: 1

tip...

You may be lucky enough to find some fabric that looks like the foliage on the block, in which case you can practically ignore the numbering system!

Prepare the Background Fabric

1 Sew the sky and water fabrics together with a ¼" seam. Press the seam open for less bulk.

2 Using freezer paper, trace the top edge of the foreground dark portion (bushes and lanterns). Lay this on the top edge of the cut foreground fabric; iron in place. Iron a 2" strip of fusible web onto the back of the fabric.

3 Cut out the foreground edge on the traced lines. Remove the freezer paper and the protective paper on the back.

4 Place the foreground edge at the water's edge, with the bushes and lanterns overlapping the sky (see photo and pattern for exact placement); iron in place.

5 Trace the large trunk shape on the right of the pattern and the other palm tree shapes on freezer paper; iron onto the fabric and apply fusible web.

6 Cut the trunks out on the traced lines; apply to the background (see photo and pattern for exact placement).

7 Sew the framing border side strips to the sides of the background fabric. Press the seams toward the borders.

8 Sew the framing border top and bottom strips to the top and bottom of the background fabric. Press the seams toward the borders.

9 Sew the second border side strips to the sides of the panel. Press the seams outward.

10 Sew the second border top and bottom strips to the top and bottom of the panel. Press the seams outward.

Prepare the background fabric.

Prepare the Palm Tree Fronds

1 Trace the palm fronds without tracing around all the pointed edges. Your tracing should look like a large leaf.

2 Draw a line in the middle of the leaf to give you a guideline on how far toward the middle of the leaf to cut the individual fringes.

3 Cut from the outside edge toward the center guideline. Make the cuts about 1" apart in a "V" shape.

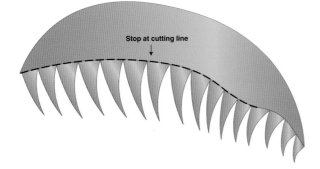

Create the fringed palm frond, starting with the leaf shape.

Trace the Pieces and Build the Block

Follow the instructions in Chapter 3 to trace the remaining pieces and assemble the block.

Machine Appliqué

Note: Use an open toe presser foot for machine appliqué. You can use a neutral-color bobbin thread or one to match your top thread.

1 Place a piece of tear-away stabilizer underneath the block; this will keep the stitching flat and smooth and will keep the satin stitches from "tunneling" the fabric.

2 Using the appropriate thread color, outline the leaves.

3 Blanket stitch around the light green leaves for more texture.

4 Satin stitch around the other leaves and the tree trunks.

Blanket stitch on the light green leaves to give it a rough texture.

Satin stitch around the foliage.

Finish the Quilt

Add a sparkly effect to the flames with crystals.

1 Using a pair of long-handled tweezers, grab the stabilizer and tear it away. To prevent the stitches from loosening as you tear away the stabilizer, hold the stitching line with your finger and thumb to keep it firm.

2 Set this block aside if you are making a larger wallhanging quilt until you have all the blocks for the quilt completed. Or, finish it as a single wallhanging unit by layering it with batting and a backing, and following the quilting instructions on page 40.

3 As an option, apply some yellow or light orange beads or pre-glued crystals on and around the flames from the torches for a little added sparkle.

hotel del coronado

San Diego, California

Postcard of the Hotel Del Coronado.

The Hotel Del, as it is known locally, is an old, Victorian-style building on Coronado Island in the San Diego Bay. Two Midwestern businessmen bought the undeveloped land in 1885, subdivided, sold off lots to recoup their cash, and built a fishing and hunting resort. It opened in 1888 and underwent a huge restoration a few years ago. It is a dramatic presence in the area, and well known for its background as a movie set, for its notable guests, and especially in October for its ghost! This pattern is designed for a block on point, or a square set on a diagonal orientation that produces a commanding appearance.

FABRICS

- Fat quarter of blue for the sky

- ⅛ yd. each of dark red, medium red, medium-light red and light red for the roof

- ⅛ yd. each of white, off-white, light gray and gray for the building

- Scrap of dark for the inside of the windows

- Scraps of white for the little windows

- Scrap of lace or tulle for the balcony

- Scraps of tropical flower print for fussy cut flowers

- Scrap of palm tree print for fussy cut palm trees

- Fat quarter of white for the first border

- Fat quarter of blue for the setting triangles

- Scrap of flag fabric for the flag at the top of the building

- ½ yd. blue for the large side triangles

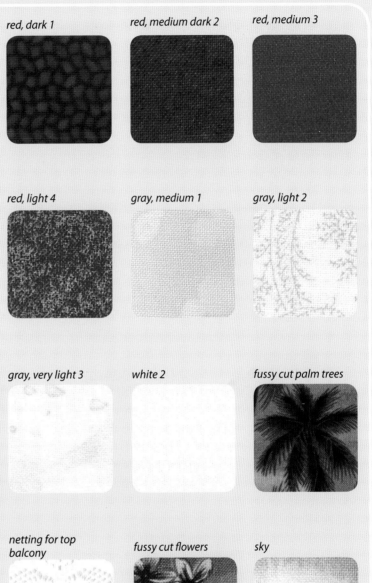

red, dark 1   *red, medium dark 2*   *red, medium 3*

red, light 4   *gray, medium 1*   *gray, light 2*

gray, very light 3   *white 2*   *fussy cut palm trees*

netting for top balcony

fussy cut flowers   *sky*

CUTTING INSTRUCTIONS

From the sky fabric, cut:
- One 14½" square on point, or on the diagonal, being aware of directional fabrics

From the roof fabric, cut:
- According to pattern

From the building fabrics, cut:
- According to pattern

From the inside window fabric, cut:
- According to pattern

From the little window fabric, cut:
- According to pattern

From the balcony lace, cut:
- One 1½" x 4" rectangle

From the flower fabric, cut:
Note: The number of flowers needed depends on the individual size of the flowers and your creative placement.
- According to print (fussy cut the flowers); add fusible web to the back before fussy cutting

From the palm tree fabric, cut:
- According to the print (fussy cut the trees)

From the first border fabric, cut:
- Four 1¾" x 14½" strips

From the setting triangles fabric, cut:
- One 16" x 16" square; cut it twice on the diagonal

Choosing Fabric

When choosing sky fabric, use a process of elimination to select the right sky that will complement the hotel. The focus of the piece is the hotel so you can eliminate any skies that are too busy and do not allow the hotel to be seen clearly. You can also eliminate any skies that have colors that are too jarring a contrast to the red of the building. Keep in mind that this block is assembled on point, or on the diagonal. Take that into consideration when selecting a sky fabric that has a horizontal orientation.

Prepare the Background Fabric

1 Sew the white side border strips to the sides of the 14½" square sky background (sew opposite sides first, then the remaining sides). Press the seams toward the borders.

2 Sew one setting triangle to each border. Press the seams outward.

3 Apply the fussy cut flowers to the bottom of the quilt, gently overlapping some of the border strips.

Trace the Pieces and Build the Block

1 Follow the instructions in Chapter 3 to trace the pieces and assemble the block.

2 To make the little flag, follow the instructions on page 91.

Flowers extend beyond the background into the border of the Hotel Del Coronado.

Machine Appliqué

Note: Use an open toe presser foot for machine appliqué. You can use a neutral-color bobbin thread or one to match your top thread.

1 Place a piece of tear-away stabilizer underneath the block; this will keep the stitching flat and smooth and will keep the satin stitches from "tunneling" the fabric.

2 Using thread in shades of red, outline the rooftop of the building with satin stitching.

3 Using white thread, outline the white portions of the building with satin stitching.

4 Using metallic thread, outline the flagpole at the top with satin stitching.

5 Free-motion stitch the top of the palm trees with gold thread.

6 Free-motion stitch the palm tree trunks with brown thread.

7 Use a decorative stitch and shiny thread for the flowers.

Add the Balcony

1 With an air or water erasable pen, draw the outside lines for the balcony, refering to the pattern. Cut a piece of netting or lace larger than the area being covered.

2 Following the traced lines, sew the netting or lace using monofilament thread and a small, narrow zigzag stitch.

3 Using small scissors, snip the excess net or lace away.

Finish the Quilt

1 Using a pair of long-handled tweezers, grab the stabilizer and tear it away. To prevent the stitches from loosening as you tear away the stabilizer, hold the stitching line with your finger and thumb to keep it firm.

2 Set this block aside if you are making a larger wallhanging quilt until you have all the blocks for the quilt completed. Or, finish it as a single wallhanging unit by layering it with batting and a backing, and following the quilting instructions on page 40.

3 As an option, add beads or crystals to the flowers or windows for additional sparkle.

washington monument on the 4th of july

Washington, D.C.

This building is one of the most highly recognized memorial buildings in the world. It was designed by Robert Mills and construction began in 1848. Construction stopped when the money was exhausted, and it was not resumed until public interest was revived in 1876. The monument opened to the public in 1888 and is made of 36,000 pieces of marble and granite. Our block, however, will be constructed with fabric!

FABRICS

- Fat quarter of dark blue for the sky

- Fat quarter of dark green for the ground and trees

- Scrap of white for the front of the building

- Scrap of gray for the side of the building

- Scrap of yellow for the windows at the top

- Scrap of fireworks print for fussy cut fireworks

- Fat quarter of yellow for the framing border

- Fat quarter of a complimentary bright for the second border

- Fat quarter of blue for the third border

sky

grass and trees

building

tiny top windows

fireworks

CUTTING INSTRUCTIONS

From the sky fabric, cut:
- One 11" x 16" rectangle

From the grass fabric, cut:
- According to pattern

From the white scrap for the building, cut:
- According to pattern

From the gray scrap for the building, cut:
- According to pattern

From the yellow scrap for the top windows, cut:
- According to pattern

From the fireworks fabric, cut:
- Fussy cut 3-4 large fireworks and 8-12 small fireworks

From the framing border fabric, cut:
- Two 1" x 14½" side border strips
- Two 1" x 12" top and bottom border strips

From the second border fabric, cut:
- Two 2¾" x 16" side border strips
- Two 2¾" x 15¾" top and bottom border strips

Prepare the Background Fabric

1 Sew the framing border side strips to the sides of the background fabric. Press the seams toward the borders.

2 Sew the framing border top and bottom strips to the top and bottom of the background fabric. Press the seams toward the borders.

3 Sew the second border side strips to the sides of the panel. Press the seams outward.

4 Sew the second border top and bottom strips to the top and bottom of the panel. Press the seams outward.

5 Sew the third border side strips to the sides of the panel. Press the seams outward.

6 Sew the third border top and bottom strips to the top and bottom of the panel. Press the seams outward.

Trace the Pieces and Build the Block

Follow the instructions in Chapter 3 to trace the pieces and assemble the block.

Cut out the patterns.

Place the monument piece on the background fabric.

Machine Appliqué

Note: Use an open toe presser foot for machine appliqué. You can use a neutral-color bobbin thread or one to match your top thread.

1 Place a piece of tear-away stabilizer underneath the block; this will keep the stitching flat and smooth and will keep the satin stitches from "tunneling" the fabric.

2 Outline the building using white embroidery thread and a small satin stitch. Don't forget to satin stitch around the little windows at the top.

3 Add one or more flags around the base of the monument.

4 Sew on the fireworks; add one or two fireworks (cut in half) to appear from behind the monument (half circles on each side of the monument, making sure to align them).

FLAG OPTION

If your flag fabric contains flags that are too large in proportion to the monument, you can create the illusion of a smaller flag quite simply. Decide on the size you want for your flag by drawing a rectangle on a piece of paper, and cutting it out. The rectangle can be made with wavy lines to look more like a waving flag. Place the paper with the cutout on your flag fabric. Position the cutout just so the edge of the blue portion of the flag shows in the corner. The small blue/white star portion and some red and white stripes will give you the illusion of a smaller flag. Apply fusible to the back of the flag and use it on your block. You can use one or many small flags.

1 *Example of a flag print that is too large in scale.*

2 *Cut out a smaller flag pattern.*

3 *Place the pattern on the flag print fabric.*

4 *Cut out the flag. The end result is the appearance of a flag, in the correct proportion.*

Finish the Quilt

1 Using a pair of long-handled tweezers, grab the stabilizer and tear it away. To prevent the stitches from loosening as you tear away the stabilizer, hold the stitching line with your finger and thumb to keep it firm.

2 Set this block aside if you are making a larger wallhanging quilt until you have all the blocks for the quilt completed. Or, finish it as a single wallhanging unit by layering it with batting and a backing, and following the quilting instructions on page 40. *Note:* This block does not lend itself to heavy quilting, just around fireworks and a little in the sky.

FIREWORKS OPTION

If you were not able to find a fireworks print, you can make your own! First, choose several different colors of scraps. Hand draw various-sized circles on the fabric using a chalk pencil. Fireworks come in all colors, and often many colors in one burst. Look at pictures of fireworks to help gain perspective. Sew the circles to the fabric. Because your background sky is dark, you should use light metallic threads. Free-motion stitching in a large Z formation around the circles gives the impression of the bursting embers. Add a few "whoosh" marks (single stitching lines that curve gently from near the top of the block downward toward the earth).

mission san xavier del bac

Tucson, Arizona

This lovely Catholic church is the oldest one in the United States, founded originally in 1692. In 1783, the church that exists today was built, but through the years decay took over and local American Indians took furnishings into their homes to preserve them. The door was always open, so the church was soon taken over by birds. Help came in 1859 when repairs began and a priest was assigned to serve there. To this day, it still serves the local parish. It is located in the desert south of Tucson and is pristine white, thus, the locals refer to it as the "Dove of the Desert."

Photos of Mission San Xavier del Bac.

FABRICS

- Fat quarter of blue for the sky
- Fat quarter of beige or light brown for the ground at the front of the building
- Scraps of brown for the balcony
- Scrap of lace for the upper balcony
- Scraps of cactus print for the fussy-cut cactus

- Scraps of green for the foliage
- Scraps of gray and mottled gray for the stones in front
- Fat quarter of white for the framing border
- Fat quarter of black for the second border
- Fat quarter of beige for the third border

bush

bush

bush

bush

building

building

building

cactus

door and balcony

center building

stones

sand

shadowed building

towers

sky

balcony railing

CUTTING INSTRUCTIONS

From the sky fabric, cut:
- One 10" x 9½" rectangle

From the ground fabric, cut:
- One 10" x 5" rectangle

From the brown balcony scraps, cut:
- According to pattern

From the upper balcony lace, cut:
- According to pattern

From the cactus print, cut:
- Fussy-cut cactus (as many as desired)

From the green foliage scraps, cut:
- According to pattern

From the gray stone scraps, cut:
- According to pattern

From the framing border fabric cut:
- Two 1½" x 14" side border strips
- Two 1½" x 12" top and bottom border strips

From the second border fabric, cut:
- Two 1" x 15" side border strips
- Two 1" x 12" top and bottom border strips

From the third border fabric, cut:
- Two 2¾" x 19" side border strips
- Two 2¾" x 17" top and bottom border strips

Prepare the Background Fabric

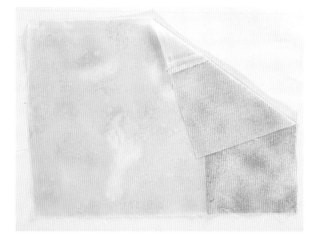

Prepare the background.

1 Sew the sky and ground fabric together with a ¼" seam. Press the seam open.

2 Sew the framing border side strips to the sides of the background fabric. Press the seams toward the borders.

3 Sew the framing border top and bottom strips to the top and bottom of the background fabric. Press the seams toward the borders.

4 Sew the second border side strips to the sides of the panel. Press the seams outward.

5 Sew the second border top and bottom strips to the top and bottom of the panel. Press the seams outward.

6 Sew the third border side strips to the sides of the panel. Press the seams outward.

7 Sew the third border top and bottom strips to the top and bottom of the panel. Press the seams outward.

Trace the Pieces and Build the Block

Follow the instructions in Chapter 3 to trace the pieces and assemble the block.

Machine Appliqué

Note: Use an open toe presser foot for machine appliqué. You can use a neutral-color bobbin thread or one to match your top thread.

1 Place a piece of tear-away stabilizer underneath the block; this will keep the stitching flat and smooth and will keep the satin stitches from "tunneling" the fabric.

2 Using the appropriate thread color to match the parts of the building, satin stitch to outline each part.

Add the Balcony

Use lace trim for the balcony.

1 With an air or water erasable pen, draw the outside lines for the balcony, refering to the pattern. Cut a piece of lace larger than the area being covered.

2 Following the traced lines, sew the lace using monofilament thread and a small, narrow zigzag stitch.

3 Using small scissors, snip away the excess net or lace.

Add the Cactus Flowers

Add the fussy-cut catus flowers to the block.

1 Place the cactus flowers on the block. Using a green thread and a straight stitch, sew the long leaves to the block.

2 Using a gold or variegated thread, use a decorative or free-motion stitch on the flowers.

tip...

Cactus flowers cut from a print fabric can do a lot to create the feel of the desert. Many fabrics feature a Southwest desert motif with cactus plants. You can also draw your plant. If you are not into drawing, buy some children's coloring books to find just what you need for that cactus.

Add the Lettering

Trace the mirror imaged letters onto the paper side of fusible web.

Sew the lettering onto the block using monofilament thread.

Note: For the Tucson Mission, you may opt to include the lettering on the block. Although the mission is a favorite site in the Tucson area, many outside the Tuscon area do not recognize it. Including the lettering on the block informs people what it is and where it is located.

1 Print the lettering in reverse (mirror image) with your computer word processing program. Make the letters any font and size desired. Usually, the printer has an option to print a transfer print (this means you are printing something on special paper for transferring, like if you need to place the paper pattern face down and iron it on to a shirt). Some printers do not have this feature. If not, try a graphics program that has the option to make a mirror image of your lettering.

2 Print the mirror image.

3 Trace the image onto the paper side of the fusible web.

4 Press the traced letters onto the wrong side of your chosen fabric.

5 Cut out the letters individually.

6 Place the letters on your block where desired. Sew around each letter or through the center of each letter with clear monofilament thread.

Finish the Quilt

1 Using a pair of long-handled tweezers, grab the stabilizer and tear it away. To prevent the stitches from loosening as you tear away the stabilizer, hold the stitching line with your finger and thumb to keep it firm.

2 Set this block aside if you are making a larger wallhanging quilt until you have all the blocks for the quilt completed. Or, finish it as a single wallhanging unit by layering it with batting and a backing, and following the quilting instructions on page 40.

3 Visualizing your light source coming from the left, use a permanent fabric marker to draw an oblong shape on the fabric to the right of each stone, with the left end of the oblong shape just touching the stone's bottom. Fill in the oblong shape with the marker.

4 Starting at the side of the stone, draw a line on the stone from the oblong shadow up the side of the stone, stopping before you reach the top.

5 Starting at the bottom of the stone, draw a line on the stone from the oblong shadow along the bottom edge, about halfway across the bottom.

Add shadows to the stone using a permanent fabric marker.

victorian homes

Alamo Park, San Francisco, California

There is something nostalgic about those wonderfully embellished Victorian homes in San Francisco. The gingerbread trim on each one is different and fascinating. Using lace for that trim on the houses came to me while I was dreading cutting out the intricate pieces. I found the right laces at the bridal section of several fabric stores, sparking the curiosity of the clerks as to just why I was buying all those little 1/8 yard pieces!

FABRICS

- Fat quarter of blue for the sky
- Fat quarter of green for the grass
- Fat eighth of green for the trees
- Scraps of blue, gray, black and brown for the rooftops and steps
- Scraps of lace for the gingerbread trim
- Scraps of yellow, green, blue and beige for the houses
- 1½ yd. lace for the outside border trim, 3½" wide
- Fat quarter of black for the framing border
- Fat quarter of pale yellow for the second border

House A

House B

House C

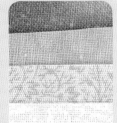

sky, cement, windows, bushes/trees

House D

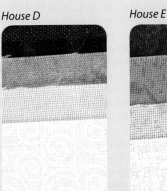

House E

CUTTING INSTRUCTIONS

From the sky fabric, cut:
- One 12½" x 11" rectangle

From the grass fabric, cut:
- One 2" x 11"

From the tree fabric, cut:
- According to pattern

From the rooftop and steps scraps, cut:
- According to pattern

From the gingerbread trim lace, cut:
- According to pattern

From the black framing border fabric, cut:
- Two 1½" x 11" side border strips
- Two 1½" x 14¼" top and bottom border strips

From the pale yellow second border fabric, cut:
- Two 3½" x 12¾" side border strips
- Two 3½" x 19¾" top and bottom border strips

From the lace, cut and set aside:
- Two 3½" x 12¾" side pieces
- Two 3½" x 19¾" top and bottom pieces

Prepare the Background Fabric

1 Sew the sky and grass fabric together with a ¼" seam. Press the seam open.

2 Sew the framing border side strips to the sides of the background fabric. Press the seams toward the borders.

3 Sew the framing border top and bottom strips to the top and bottom of the background fabric. Press the seams toward the borders.

4 Sew the second border side strips to the sides of the panel. Press the seams outward.

5 Sew the second border top and bottom strips to the top and bottom of the panel. Press the seams outward.

Trace the Pieces and Build the Block

Follow the instructions in Chapter 3 to trace the pieces and assemble the block

tip...

Make the houses easier by tracing House A pieces first, then assemble that house and set it aside. Next, assemble House B. Add it to right side of House A and set both aside. Continue with the houses in this manner. Since the houses have unprotected fusible web on the back, be sure to place them on another pressing sheet or a plastic bag so they won't gather lint or stick to something else.

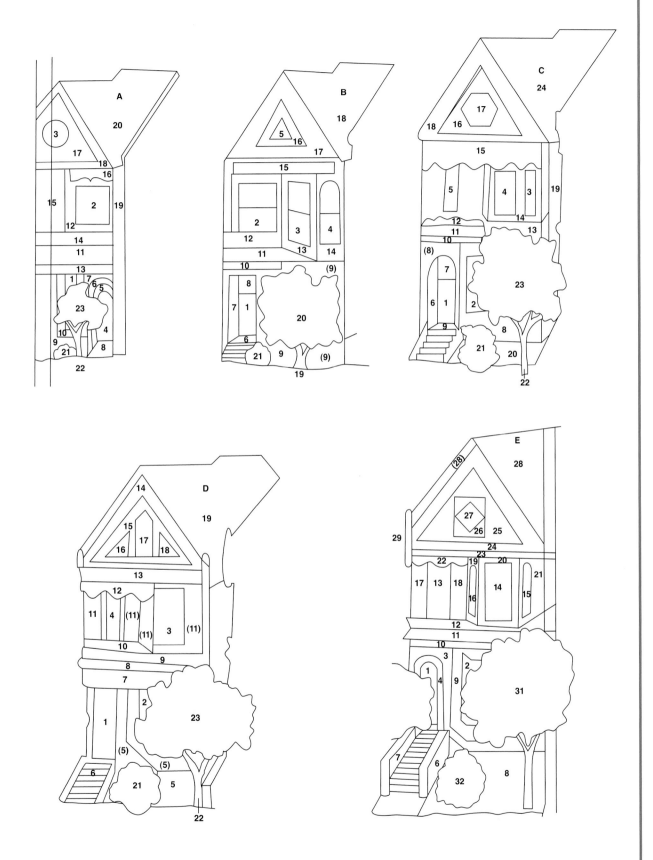

Trace Houses A–E separately, then assemble them on the pressing sheet.

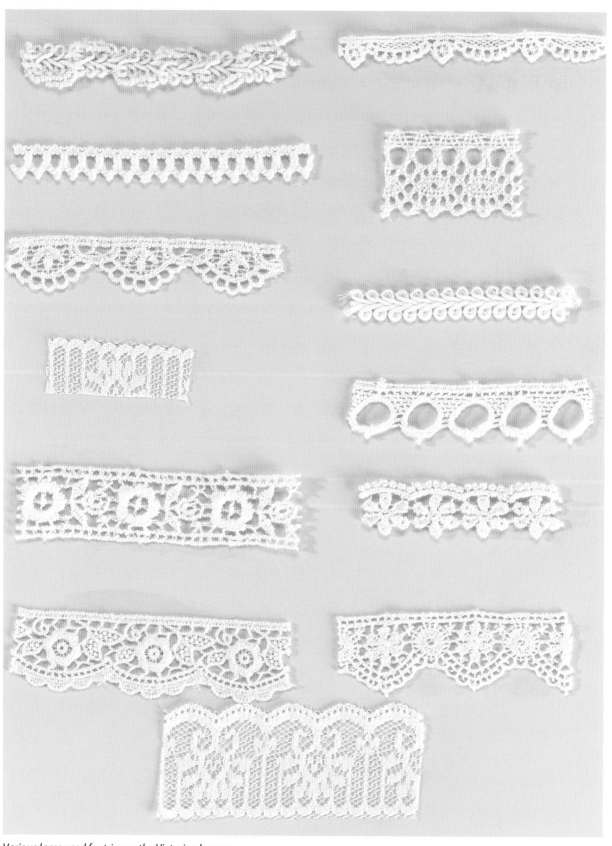

Various laces used for trim on the Victorian houses.

Machine Appliqué

Note: Use an open toe presser foot for machine appliqué. You can use a neutral-color bobbin thread or one to match your top thread.

1 Place a piece of tear-away stabilizer underneath the block; this will keep the stitching flat and smooth and will keep the satin stitches from "tunneling" the fabric.

2 Using thread colors that match or blend with the house colors, outline the rooftops, buildings, doors, windows and steps with a narrow satin stitch.

3 Add the lace gingerbread trim using clear monofilament thread and a short, narrow zigzag stitch.

4 Use a decorative or blanket stitch on the trees and edge of the grass with green thread.

Finish the Quilt

1 Using a pair of long-handled tweezers, grab the stabilizer and tear it away. To prevent the stitches from loosening as you tear away the stabilizer, hold the stitching line with your finger and thumb to keep it firm.

2 Set this block aside if you are making a larger wallhanging quilt until you have all the blocks for the quilt completed. Or, finish it as a single wallhanging unit by layering it with batting and a backing, and following the quilting instructions on page 40.

3 Add the lace border trim before you apply the binding. Pin the lace strips in place, aligning them on the raw edges to the outside edges of the quilt. The lace will be attached as you sew on the binding.

GALLERY

The collection of quilts on these pages were made by my students and me using my fusible web and machine appliqué techniques. My quilts were inspired by my travels and photographs of those places I love to visit. My students brought their favorite photographs to class and captured those fondly remembered moments and places for their own distinctive quilts.

Celebrate San Diego. 63" x 61". Designed and created by Betty Alofs.

San Francisco Quilt. 55½" x 55½". Designed and created by Betty Alofs.

*The Immaculata Church at the University of San Diego. 12½" x 12½".
Designed and created by Jean Nagy, Poway, Calif.*

California Missions. 52" x 73½". Designed and created by Betty Alofs.

TEXAS. 46" x 46". Designed and created by Betty Alofs.

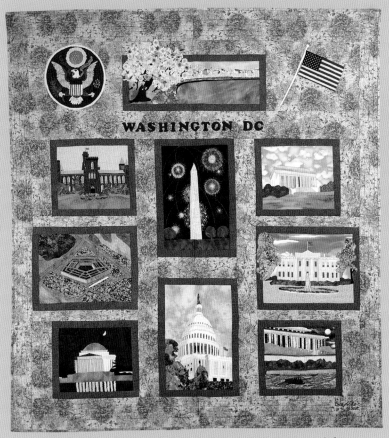

Washington, DC. 56" x 59". Designed and created by Betty Alofs.

Aloha Hawaii. 58" x 62". Designed and created by Betty Alofs.

Hawaiian Critters. 35" x 29". Designed and created by Betty Alofs.

Eureka, CA Table Bluff Lighthouse Tower. 14" x 18".
Designed and created by Betty Alofs.

The Presidio. 13½" x 19". Designed and created by Betty Alofs.

Welcome to Our Home. 33½" x 19". Designed and created by Betty Alofs.

The Chapel at Asilomar Conference Grounds, Pacific Grove, Calif. 20½" x 15½". Designed and created by Betty Alofs.

Vacation Quilt. 28" x 35". Designed and created by Carol Fredericks, Carlsbad, Calif.

*Our Cabin in the Woods. 32" x 29".
Designed and created by Janet Haas,
Ramona, Calif.*

My Home. 17" x 17".
Designed and created by
Julie McKinney, El Cajon, Calif.

Ballintuber Abbey, Castlebar, Ireland. 13½" x 11¾".
Designed and created by Jean Nagy, Poway, Calif.

Star of India Maritime Museum on San Diego Bay. 8" x 19".
Designed and created by Elise McKibben, Carlsbad, Calif.

Covered Bridge. 22½" x 19¼". Designed and created by Janis Bennett Salcfas, Elizabeth Lake, Calif.

*Carlsbad Windmill. 8" x 19".
Designed and created by Elise
McKibben, Carlsbad, Calif.*

Pemequid Lighthouse, Maine.
26½" x 28½".
Designed and created by
Judy Shephard, San Diego, Calif.

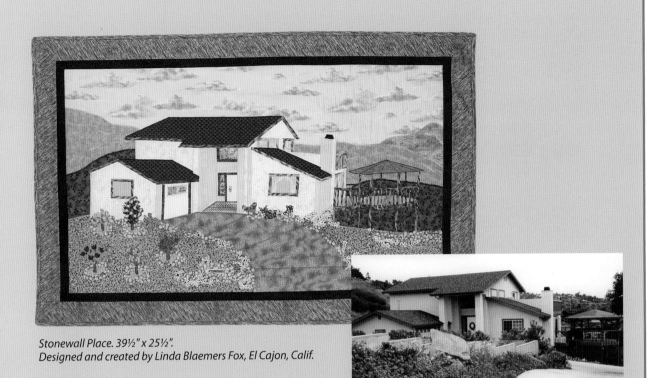

Stonewall Place. 39½" x 25½".
Designed and created by Linda Blaemers Fox, El Cajon, Calif.

El Cajon, CA Historical Society Quilt. 56" x 70". Designed and created by Betty Alofs, Joylene Bouma, Lucille Boyd, Georgette Del 'Orco, Marilyn Hanson, Janet Harris, Charlene Hauri, Pia Parrish, Daniela Stout and Liz Schmidt. Quilted by Susanne Fagot. This quilt was made as a gift to the city of El Cajon.

RESOURCES

Contributors

I used the following products to make the quilts in this book.
Thank you to these companies for providing superior materials.

Bear Thread Designs
P.O. Box 1452
Highland, TX 77562
(281) 462-0661
www.bearthreaddesigns.com
BearTD@Hotmail.com
The Appliqué Pressing Sheet

Pfaff Sewing Machines
P.O. Box 458012
Westlake, OH 44145
www.pfaffusa.com.
(440) 808-6550
Available at shops throughout the world.
Pfaff Quilt Expression Sewing Machine

Sakura of America
www.gellyroll.com
Available at art supply stores, craft stores, quilt shops.
Pigma® Micron® Pens

Sharpie®
www.sharpie.com
Available at office supply stores, art stores, drug stores.
Permanent Ink Fine Point Marker; Permanent Ink Ultra Fine Point Marker

Sulky® of America
P.O. Box 494129
Port Charlotte, FL 33949-4129
(800) 874-4115
(941) 743-4634 fax
www.sulky.com
info@sulky.com
Embroidery, cotton and metallic threads; Tear Easy™ Stabilizer

The Warm™ Company
954 E. Union Street
Seattle, WA 98122
(800) 234-WARM
(206) 320-9276
www.warmcompany.com
info@warmcompany.com
Lite Steam-a-Seam 2® Fusible Web; Warm & Natural® Batting

P3 Designs
www.p3designs.com
Ultimate Appliqué Template Paper

Resources

Annie's Attic
1 Annie Lane
Big Sandy, TX 75755
(800) 582-6643
www.anniesattic.com

Clotilde, LLC
P.O. Box 7500
Big Sandy, TX 75755-7500
(800) 772-2891
www.clotilde.com

Connecting Threads
P.O. Box 870760
Vancouver, WA 98687-7760
(800) 574-6454
www.ConnectingThreads.com

Home Sew
P.O. Box 4099
Bethlehem, PA 18018-0099
(800) 344-4739
www.homesew.com

Keepsake Quilting
Route 25
P.O. Box 1618
Center Harbor, NH 03226-1618
(800) 438-5464
www.keepsakequilting.com

Krause Publications
(888) 457-2873
www.krause.com

Nancy's Notions
333 Beichl Ave.
P.O. Box 683
Beaver Dam, WI 53916-0683
(800) 833-0690
www.nancysnotions.com

about the author

Betty Alofs was born in Washington, D.C. and grew up in Maryland. She married, had five children, and later went to work for the government at the Naval Sea Systems Command in Arlington, Va. After working there for 10 years, she and her children made the big move to San Diego, Calif., where she worked for government contractors as an Administrative Officer/Technical Editor. She and her last husband reside in Lakeside, Calif.

Betty's introduction to sewing came early, as she was taught by her mother, and learned from the home economics class at school. She sewed clothing for herself, and, after her first marriage, for her children. Gradually, she gave up making garments when it became more economical to purchase ready-made clothing.

In 1989, Betty discovered the world of quilting through the purchase of a quilt kit complete with fabric, pattern and instructions through a magazine offer. After completing this first quilt, she decided make another, but this time chose her own fabrics. The fabric store didn't have exactly the right cottons, but to her amazement and delight, she discovered there were specialty shops for quilters! What a find!

She immediately began visiting shops, taking classes and making more and more quilts. This led to further exploration, finding shops everywhere, attending quilt shows and participating in several local guilds. After an early retirement from her editorial job, she began teaching locally and designing her own quilts, leading to the establishment of her at-home business of designing patterns for pictorial quilts. Some of Betty's accomplishments include:

- Completion of the Quilt in a Day Teacher Training Seminar in January, 1998
- Attendance at the C&T Teacher's Retreat, 1999, 2000, 2002 and 2003
- Established her home business Betty A's Designs, 2000
- Nominated for Teacher of the Year, sponsored by The Professional Quilter, 2001
- Quilts featured in the book, "Lone Star Quilts and Beyond," by Jan Krentz
- Quilts featured in the book, "Hunter Star Quilts and Beyond," by Jan Krentz
- Quilt featured in the book, "Diamond Quilts and Beyond," by Jan Krentz
- Quilt featured in the book, "Shoreline Quilts," by Cyndy Rymer
- Quilt featured in America From the Heart, 2001
- Quilt Juried at AQS Show, Paducah, Ky., 2001
- Quilt juried at Quilt and Sewing Fest, Special Exhibit " Down by the Sea" at Myrtle Beach, S.C., 2002
- Quilt juried at AQS Show, Paducah, Ky., 2002
- Featured Artist, Tucson Quilter's Guild Silver Salute Quilt Show, 2003
- Authored an article in The Professional Quilter Quarterly, 2003
- Featured in an article in Sampler Quilts, a Harris Publication, Issue #42, 2003
- Featured in an article in Quilting Professional, 2003
- Authored an article in The Appliqué Society newsletter, Fall, 2003
- Appeared in a segment on America Quilts Creatively, PBS TV, 2004
- Appeared in a field segment on Simply Quilts, HGTV, 2005